The
Siberian
Husky

An Owner's Guide To

A HAPPY HEALTHY PET

Howell Book House

Howell Book House

An imprint of Turner Publishing Company
4507 Charlotte Avenue, Suite 100
Nashville, TN 37209

Library of Congress Cataloging-in-Publication Data
Sikora-Siino,Betsy.
The Siberian Husky: an owner's guide to a happy,healthy pet/Betsy Sikora-Siino.
p. cm.
Includes bibliographical references
ISBN 0-87605-395-9
ISBN: 978-1-68442-432-0 (pbk)
1. Siberian huskies(Dogs). I. Title. II. Series.
SF429.S65S56 1996, 2001   95-47934
636.7'3—dc20   CIP
Manufactured in the United States of America
10 9
SF429.S65S56 1996

Series Director: Dominique Devito
Series Assistant Director: Ariel Cannon
Book Design: Michele Laseau
Cover Design: IrisJeromnimon
l Ilustration:JeffYesh
Photography:

Cover:Joan Balzarini, puppy by Judith Strom
Courtesy of the American Kennel Club: 15, 17,20, 21
Courtesy of Ken-L Ration: 93
Joan Balzarini: 8,14,46,66,96
Mary Bloom: 96,136,145
Buckinghamhill American Cocker Spaniels: 148
Sian Cox: 134
Dr. Ian Dunbar: 98,IOI,103,I ll,116--117, 122,123,127
Dan Lyons: 96
Cathy Merrithew: 129
Liz Palika: I33
Susan Rezy: II,12,48,57,62,81,96--97,136,145
Karrin Winter/Dale Churchill: 5,6,24,31,53,54,58,59,61
Paulette Braun/Pets by Paulette: 7,38,41,55,96
Scott McKiernan/Zuma: 22,44,70,134
Judith Strom: 26,27,28,29,96,107,110,128,130,135,137,139,140,144,149,150 Ted Schiffman/Animal Images: 40,43,76

Production Team: Trudy BrownJama Carter,Kathleen Caulfield,Trudy Coler, Amy DeAngelis, Pete Fornatale,Matt Hannafin,Kathy Iwasaki,Vic Peterson, Terri Sheehan, Marvin Van Tiem, and Kathleen Varanese

Contents

Welcome
to the
World
of the

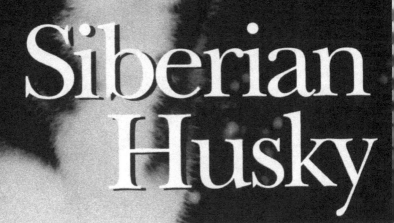

part one

Siberian Husky

External Features of the Siberian Husky

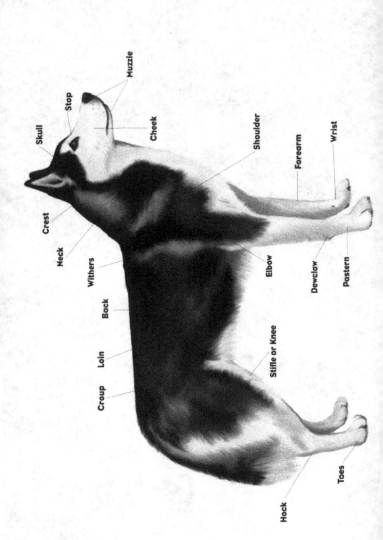

chapter 1

What

Is a

Siberian

Husky?

The Siberian Husky is a dog everyone knows. Although it is not *the* most popular pet, it is one of the most well-known American dog breeds, even among those who really don't know dogs. The reason is simple: When someone offhandedly throws out the generic term "husky" or hears of a sled dog race in Alaska, invariably the image of the Siberian Husky, a blue-eyed dog that looks like a wolf, takes shape within the mind's eye.

Despite obvious similarities in appearance and a shared affinity for howling, the Siberian Husky is no closer to the wolf than is any other domestic dog. He does share, however, an intimate knowledge of the wilderness with his wild cousin, for both have evolved in some of the harshest, most remote regions on earth.

A Strong Survivor

From such an environment has sprung a dog with speed, endurance and a friendly attitude that somehow belies the animal's great athletic ability. That dog is, of course, the Siberian Husky—the dog harnessed to a primitive sled, mushed by a fur-clad Eskimo across the frozen tundra, immortalized by Jack London in *The Call of the Wild*—the dog that carries our imaginations to the top of the world where only the fittest survive.

The Husky's eyes entrance all who look at them; they can be brown, blue or even one of each color.

Despite his great beauty and infectious smile, the Siberian Husky is one of those illustrious "fittest." Through human-assisted natural selection, he has proven he can happily survive almost anywhere. Yet the Siberian is shrouded in myth and legend, leaving modern humans to sort out what is real and what is fiction—something the Siberian owner must do if he or she is to become the partner this dog demands.

The Husky's Heritage

Although much of the Siberian's legend is just that, the truths of the breed at times seem mythological. The credit for these myths goes to the many people throughout history who have guided the breed's fate with wisdom and respect. Entrusted with a dog bred for an estimated three thousand years by the Chukchis of Siberia, today's American breeders, armed with the American Kennel Club (AKC) standard that dictates the ins and outs of Siberian breeding, continue to do justice to what those native breeders intended for their treasure. Were those ancient Chukchis transported forward in time, they would probably have little trouble recognizing their dogs in a gathering of twentieth-century canines.

A Big Dog in a Not-So-Big Package

What might surprise the neo-phyte viewing a Siberian Husky for the first time is the dog's rela-tively small size. How could this diminutive, almost delicate crea-ture be the grand dog of the north? the inspiration of count-less adventure fantasies? Jack London's muse?

The Siberian Husky was designed for ultimate effi-ciency, that's how. What follows is a discussion of the physical characteristics of the Siberian Husky, based on the breed's standard. For a copy of the official stan-dard, write to the American Kennel Club, 51 Madison Avenue, New York, NY 10010.

Huskies can come in all col-ors, from black to pure white, like this one.

Height According to the official standard of the breed as accepted by the American Kennel Club (AKC) and evident in most of the Siberians seen today, this high-powered athlete should stand just under two feet at the withers. Specifically, females should stand twenty to twenty-two inches, males twenty-one to twenty-three-and-one-half inches. Females should weigh thirty-five to fifty pounds, males forty-five to sixty pounds.

The Siberian Husky is quite a bit smaller than the Alaskan Malamute, another wolfy-looking Arctic breed that, despite the dramatic size differences, is often mistaken for his smaller cousin and vice versa. Nevertheless, that smaller cousin continues to amaze spectators and enthusiasts alike as one of the smallest, yet most capable dogs in the AKC's Working Group.

The Siberian's profile resembles that of the wolf.

Build The Siberian Husky is described in the standard as a "medium-sized working dog, quick and light on its feet and free and graceful in action." It is precisely this image, one the dog readily embodies, that has drawn so many people from so many cultures to this breed.

Elegant and athletic, compact and well balanced, the well-bred Siberian Husky cuts a sturdy figure with moderate bone and hard muscle, which facilitate the extraordinary strength and endurance for which the breed is known.

Engineered to move almost effortlessly across the snow and ice, the Siberian boasts straight, parallel front legs with elbows held close to the body. The hindquarters are equally straight and parallel, the thighs rich with powerful muscle to propel the dog forward with balance and precision.

Tail Assisting in that mission is the tail, well-furred (though not too well-furred or too tightly curled) and carried over the back when the dog is alert and attentive. When relaxed, the Siberian's tail is dropped. When excited, no doubt when greeting either a known family member or a new acquaintance, the Siberian's tail wags wildly like a flag flying high above his back.

Feet   Whereas the tail adds balance and is a means of communicating moods, the structure of the Siberian's feet enables the dog to move in a way that makes one think the animal must surely be running on air. To keep the Siberian stepping lightly, those feet should be oval in shape and of medium size with thick, protective pads underneath and a dense growth of hair between the pads and toes. Such accoutrements provide the dog with traction and protection from frigid climates and rugged terrain. The Siberian can thus run tirelessly in the coldest of temperatures. To watch him move with such effortless grace is to witness the ideal marriage of agility and elegance.

Breathtaking Beauty

Eyes   For most people, it's the Siberian's glacier-blue eyes that first capture their attention. But while all Siberians see through almond-shaped, almost humanly expressive eyes, not all Siberians see the world through eyes of blue.

The standard allows eyes that are brown, blue or even one of each. Particolored eyes are also acceptable. Look closely into those eyes, which have been known to unnerve if not outright frighten the uninitiated, and you may just note a hint of wanderlust smoldering within.

Head   Even with those mysterious eyes, the Siberian's expression is one of energy and exuberance and even, as the standard suggests, projects an element of mischief.

The Siberian's profile resembles that of the wolf: his muzzle medium in width, tapered to the nose; the triangular-shaped, well-furred ears with softly rounded tips positioned high on his head, alert to any new and exciting sound; teeth closed in a scissor bite, except when the jaw is open in the traditional Siberian smile.

Coat   Also unforgettable is the Siberian Husky's thick, medium-length double coat, a veritable feat of both beauty and engineering that is common to all of the northern breeds. Consisting of a soft, fluffy undercoat close to the skin covered by a sea of coarser, longer guard hairs, these two layers work in concert to insulate the dog naturally from even subzero temperatures.

When faced with such temperatures, the hair follicles in the dog's coat respond by standing erect to trap and, with the body's natural heat, warm the air in the thick undercoat. The guard hairs also protect the skin from vegetation and other environmental irritants, and as an added bonus, the coat rarely emits the doggy odor common to so many other members of the canine species. Indeed, the Siberian is a very clean breed, and he generally strives to maintain his own cleanliness almost as diligently as does a cat.

Colors   Apart from its obvious value in protecting the dog from the elements, the Siberian's coat is aesthetically irresistible as well. According to the Standard, all colors are allowed, from black to pure white (colors that determine what color the dog's nose will be), but Siberians are most frequently found in shimmering red and white, black and white, gray and white, and copper and white.

THE AMERICAN KENNEL CLUB

Familiarly referred to as "the AKC," the American Kennel Club is a nonprofit organization devoted to the advancement of purebred dogs. The AKC maintains a registry of recognized breeds and adopts and enforces rules for dog events including shows, obedience trials, field trials, hunting tests, lure coursing, herding, earthdog trials, agility and the Canine Good Citizen program. It is a club of clubs, established in 1884 and composed, today, of over 500 autonomous dog clubs throughout the United States. Each club is represented by a delegate; the delegates make up the legislative body of the AKC, voting on rules and electing directors. The American Kennel Club maintains the Stud Book, the record of every dog ever registered with the AKC, and publishes a variety of materials on purebred dogs, including a monthly magazine, books and numerous educational pamphlets. For more information, contact the AKC at the address listed in Chapter 13, "Resources," and look for the names of their publications in Chapter 12, "Recommended Reading."

This attractive coat may be complemented by a raccoon-like bandit mask that marks the face of many a Siberian. Like snowflakes, no two Siberian Huskies share identical patterns and markings. No two are alike.

Well-Balanced Soul

Also unique is the Siberian Husky's disposition, which, like the dog's size, may also surprise those who have come to know sled dogs solely through Jack London's books. In other words, despite what Mr. London's tales may tell us, this is no vicious fighting dog, no incorruptible warrior. The Siberian Husky loves everyone, and his mission in life is to ensure that everyone knows it.

The Siberian Husky was developed in one of the harshest and most remote regions of the earth.

Temperament   The well-bred Siberian Husky is balanced in both physique and disposition. As the breed's standard emphasizes, the Siberian's temperament is just as critical to the dog's identity as are his distinctive physical attributes. Furthermore, that temperament must be friendlier and gentler than any human being could ever hope to have.

Don't expect quintessential guard-dog behavior from your Siberian. This dog is driven to share all he has

11

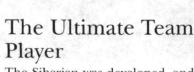
and all his owner has with anyone and everyone he happens to meet. Friendly, outgoing, gentle and alert are the words used to describe the ideal Siberian character. The Siberian in turn takes these concepts to heart as his birthright.

Your Siberian Husky should display an inherent *joie de vivre*—boundless energy indicative of a true love for life. He is a gregarious animal, raised traditionally for deadly serious work in a region where all members of the tribe, both canine and human, knew their lives hung by a thread every day. Yet the Siberian reveled in his work and in his close relationship with the people and other dogs with whom he lived and survived.

Your Siberian Husky should possess a true love for life— for work and for family.

The Ultimate Team Player

The Siberian was developed, and very successfully so, to be the ultimate team player. He thrives best in the company of people whose greatest joy is to spend a great deal of time with their dogs—and in the company of other dogs, too, a perspective no doubt sculpted by the dog's spending centuries in the pack in frigid Siberia.

The Siberian Husky, however, is not clingy or constantly hungry for human acceptance. Such a suggestion would elicit peals of laughter from any seasoned Siberian enthusiast. This dog is independent with a stubborn intelligence that can easily try the patience of even the most experienced dog trainer. Yet the Siberian will both obey and disobey with equal gusto and humor—behavior that may not be so eagerly shared by those trying to direct the dog's energy and actions into institutionalized patterns of obedience.

The Siberian is nevertheless quite sensitive to the rules of the pack—historically, he had to be to survive. While he thus extends his affection to all, he reserves his respect for only the few who earn it. One way to earn that respect is to be a firm yet gentle leader and to provide the dog with ample opportunity for adventure. As his variegated history demonstrates, the Siberian Husky, when led by a worthy leader, has always adapted well to every new situation. This adaptability is a vital facet of this ancient breed.

chapter 2

The Siberian Husky's Ancestry

Over thousands of years, the Husky and Chukchis grew to depend on each other, just as your Husky depends on you.

If a filmmaker ever attempted to tackle the story of the Siberian Husky, the resulting film would surely be epic. Three thousand years of history are not easily compressed into a few short hours of celluloid, especially when those years are filled with adventures and life-threatening challenges that would make most modern-day action heroes blanche.

What would further contribute to this film's inevitable success is that unlike most of today's action blockbusters, this one would be true. It would be useful, too, for if we take the time to contemplate the details of the Siberian's past, we begin to see the patterns. We begin to see the subtle threads come together, illuminating clearly the unique behaviors and character that are the Siberian Husky. With such insight we are thus destined to become better owners and better partners to this fine old spirit.

*The Husky
hails from a
land of ice and
snow.*

Life in Exile

For most, the thought of exile in Siberia is a nightmare. For the Siberian Husky, it is home.

This barren region of ice and snow, where countless political prisoners were sent as a cruel and unusual form of punishment, was also historically the native land of the Chukchis. That we know of these people and that they remained in the region for thousands of years is a testament to the dog that made it all happen. Without their dogs—dogs that would ultimately be named the Siberian Husky—their culture, their people, probably would not have survived.

Dog historians believe that the northern breeds—Siberian Husky, Alaskan Malamute, Samoyed and so forth—all shared a common ancestor (whether or not that ancestor was the wolf is a subject for debate that will probably never be settled). Canine historian Maxwell Riddle has spoken of the "family of the

15

northern forest," the dogs that would become our modern Nordic dogs. With such a family in their background, these breeds, though retaining certain like characteristics, diverged into their distinctive types, based on the various people who nurtured them and according to the demands of their owners' specific climates and terrains and their subsequent needs in sled dogs.

WHERE DID DOGS COME FROM?

It can be argued that dogs were right there at man's side from the beginning of time. As soon as human beings began to document their existence, the dog was among their drawings and inscriptions. Dogs were not just friends, they served a purpose: There were dogs to hunt birds, pull sleds, herd sheep, burrow after rats—even sit in laps! What your dog was originally bred to do influences the way it behaves. The American Kennel Club recognizes over 140 breeds, and there are hundreds more distinct breeds around the world. To make sense of the breeds, they are grouped according to their size or function. The AKC has seven groups:

1) Sporting, 2) Working,
3) Herding, 4) Hounds,
5) Terriers, 6) Toys,
7) Nonsporting

Can you name a breed from each group? Here's some help: (1) Golden Retriever; (2) Doberman Pinscher; (3) Collie; (4) Beagle; (5) Scottish Terrier; (6) Maltese, and (7) Dalmatian. All modern domestic dogs (*Canis familiaris*) are related, however different they look, and are all descended from *Canis lupus*, the gray wolf.

Chukchi Dogs

For the Chukchis, this meant developing a dog that would meet the very specific demands of their environment and lifestyle. The Chukchis lived in permanent settlements inland but had to travel long distances to the coast to hunt. What they then sought in their ultimate dog was a smallish, fast animal who could transport relatively light loads over long distances in the extreme sub-zero temperatures of northeast Asia. This dog also needed an extraordinarily efficient metabolism that, due to food limitations, could be sufficiently fueled on less food than one might expect for such a hardworking animal.

Equally important to the Chukchis was the dog's amenability to working in large teams; given the size of the dogs, the heavier the sled loads became, the more dogs the hunters would add to the team.

When we review the ancient lifestyle that led to the development of the Siberian Husky, and view the modern-day representatives of the breed, we see little difference in the dog that ancient cultures created for their specific needs and the dog that still lives among us today.

Although life for those early Siberians—both human and canine was harsh, the Chukchis exhibited a wisdom in their breeding practices that we would be wise to emulate today. They bred selectively for temperament as well as for physical characteristics, which explains why the Siberian Huskies are today legendary for their ability and willingness to work so well with both humans and other dogs—and their demands to be integral members of the family.

A True Coexistence

For obvious reasons, the Chukchis grew to depend on their dogs. On the trail they learned to trust their dogs' instincts, a trust modern-day Siberian Huskies continue to demand from those who choose to take to the trail with them. At home the dogs enjoyed an intimate involvement with their families, a bond that was strengthened because every member of the family, children and adults alike, was responsible for caring for the lifeline that was the dog team.

This unique relationship between dog and family thus elevated coexistence to a symbiotic art form all its own. The two species learned to read and

understand each other's body language, and the Siberian Husky's instincts, forged through that bond, have since saved countless lives on the trail—lives of people who have learned, like the Chukchis, to listen to their dogs.

Huskies are legendary for their ability to work well with people and other dogs.

In the time line of the Siberian's story, the dog was bred first for utility purposes and, therefore, for the survival of her people. This purpose established a foundation for the Siberian's future, a stability that would be instantly recognized by those who would meet the dog in the years ahead and ensure that she would survive the changes in lifestyle she would inevitably encounter.

Migrating to Alaska

Although her name evokes visions of a barren region in the extreme northeastern part of Asian Russia, the modern Siberian Husky is most readily identified with Alaska. The wheels of the breed's migration to the last frontier would begin to turn long before the actual fact, launched first by the rest of Russia's discovery of the Siberian.

For centuries, the Chukchis had remained successfully isolated from the rest of their continent, thanks to the ruggedness and frigid temperatures of Siberia. But as Russian explorers began to penetrate that barrier, they found a treasure, a best-kept secret, if you will, waiting there: the Siberian Husky. The dog's friendly temperament and unparalleled skills led them into the domain of new cultures. It was with the adventurer types they met there—gold seekers, fur traders and trappers—that Siberian Huskies began to migrate across the Bering Strait and into Alaska at the turn of the twentieth century.

In Alaska, the breed, in partnership with fortune hunters like Jack London, would encounter the new calling with which they would be identified most readily throughout the twentieth century: the sport of sled dog racing. Like the Siberians' skills themselves, this sport found its roots in utilitarian functions—namely, transportation. With no roads to speak of in winter, people required dog teams in order to travel from place to place. When those dogs proved to display exemplary skill and speed, as the Siberians frequently did, the mushers asked, why not pit them against others of such talent and see what happens?

Sled Dog Racing

It was within this atmosphere that Siberians ran their first recorded major race. It occurred in 1908 in the four-hundred-and-eight–mile All-Alaska Sweepstakes Race. The newcomers, mushed by someone unfamiliar with them, didn't win, but they made a great showing and attracted the attention of all spectators—including the gamblers in the crowd. From then on, the Siberian Husky took this budding sport by storm and within a few short years had become Alaska's premier racer.

Originally christened the Chukchi Husky—"husky" being a generic term for "sled pulling dog"—this new-comer to Alaska was obsessive about running and was long accustomed to hard work. The dog was thus the ideal candidate to get in on the dawn of sled dog racing at the beginning of the twentieth century. Although some onlookers originally scoffed at the dogs' size, their scoffs turned to praise as the breed proved their mettle and quickly earned a broad following.

Spectators and mushers alike admired Siberians for their speed, endurance, manageability and beauty. The dogs, meanwhile, took to racing and the sheer joy of running just for the fun of it, as though they knew this was the destiny for which they had been preparing for the past three thousand years.

Upheaval in Russia

At the same time, things did not bode well for the breed back home. The Revolution of 1917 began the process that would eventually transform Russia into the communist Soviet Union.

Part of the Soviet agenda was to rid the country of all symbols of wealth, and they labelled the Siberian Husky such a symbol. The Chukchis, who had jealous-ly guarded the purity of their dogs until their discovery in the nineteenth century, could hardly disagree with that assessment. In their culture, the wealthiest man had the finest dogs. Those dogs, countered the Soviets, must then be destroyed.

Fortunately, by this time a great many Siberian Huskies had been exported to the Territory of Alaska to feed the demand there for fast sled dogs, a craving that began to spread south into the United States. Mushing and the Siberian gained a foothold first in New England, then spread to other regions and even into other countries, a phenomenon that continues today.

The Siberian Husky was admired for her speed, endurance and manageability.

Show Dog/Work Dog

Her reputation grew by leaps and bounds and, in 1930, the Siberian Husky was granted recognition by the American Kennel Club (AKC). She has since enjoyed many hours of thunderous applause from dog show audiences, but all has not been fame and glitter for the twentieth-century Siberian Husky. During the early years of the twentieth century, the dogs were still called on from time to time for their Chukchi-borne skills and uses.

Then as now, the Siberian sports a friendly, smiling face. Then as now, she recognizes serious business and her role in it.

The Siberian Husky's career has included transporting mail in Alaska and Canada when, until the advent of the snowmobile and bush plane, dog team was the only way the mail could get through. The Siberian has pulled children by dog sled to school when a snowed-in schoolhouse was otherwise inaccessible, and she even served as a search-and-rescue dog in the Arctic during World War II. But the most profound example of the Siberian's role in serious work occurred in 1925 with the Great Serum Run.

The Great Serum Run

In the winter of that year, a diph-theria epidemic broke out in Nome, Alaska. Although a serum existed for the illness, there was no way of getting it from Anchorage to that distant point—until someone thought of enlisting the services of Leonhard Seppala, a Norwegian immigrant who had become one of Alaska's premier mushers, his dog of choice the Siberian Husky.

The Husky shares the same ancestor as other Northern breeds, but the Chukchi people made her the dog they needed to survive.

Seppala called his and many other teams throughout the territory to action, teams that were invariably dom-inated by Siberian Huskies. What ensued was a life-saving relay of dog teams through the Alaskan interior.

The news spread south, and practically overnight the art of mushing had become immortal throughout the world (including a lead dog named Balto, whose statue now stands in New York's Central Park). The Great Serum Run is still commemorated each year in Alaska with the running of the Iditarod from Anchorage to Nome.

The Twentieth Century Husky

Those who meet the Siberian Husky today might be thrilled to see that though the dog bears little resemblance to the fictional products of Jack London's imagination, the dog obviously shares much with the ancestral Siberians that so skillfully ensured their breed's niche in modern times.

Today the Siberian enjoys a career of many facets. She remains a powerful and very popular sled dog but has found contentment with people who neither want nor need to travel by dog sled. She has become a popular show dog (too popular say those who wish to guard her from the dangers of overbreeding) and a valued partner in such recreational activities as cross-country skiing, skijoring (an activity in which a single dog pulls a person on skis) and virtually any other sport in which dogs play active roles.

Today's Husky excels at dog shows, mushing events and as a true family friend.

Today the Siberian Husky no longer dominates world-class racing events but has contributed substantially to the dog that now does: the Alaskan Husky. The Alaskan Husky is essentially a mix of dogs, selected for breeding based on working abilities rather than on a physical standard. This dog tends to win the Iditarod and the other major long-distance races each year; but given her speed, endurance and smallish size, the Alaskan Husky is unmistakably descended from the Siberian.

A Natural Musher

Mushing remains the Siberian's greatest calling, of course, and she has entered the increasingly popular world of recreational mushing with a vengeance. As new owners discover the addictive properties of the breed and realize they simply must own more than one, recreational mushing, where they may put their dogs to work together in the calling for which they were bred, is the next logical step.

On a more formal level, the Siberian excels best in mid-distance races, often in teams as large as twenty dogs. Because of the breed's size and special talents, they just naturally work well together.

Those unfamiliar with the art of mushing and the dogs who love it are often inclined to place themselves in what they believe to be the sled dog's booties (paw-sized slippers the dogs wear in extreme conditions) and deem the sport cruel. The dogs, of course, have a different opinion, evident in the uncontrollable excitement and wails of joy that emerge as soon as the musher approaches the team with harness in hand.

Cruel treatment in the Siberian's eyes is being the dog who is left at home. Pulling a sled through the snow with a team of her best friends, her human leader at the helm, is what the Siberian Husky was born for. For some, it is what they live for. This was true for their ancestors, and it holds true just as profoundly today.

chapter 3

The **World**
According to the
Siberian
Husky

WANTED: Single black-and-white, blue-eyed dog with a love of snow and running, seeks human family with interest in same. Salary no issue but must be rich with recreational time and affection—and possess a good vacuum cleaner. Fluency in canine body language a definite plus. Couch potatoes need not apply.

If a Siberian Husky were to place a classified ad for the ideal owner, it would probably sound somewhat like the ad above. In truth, the Siberian is actually looking for an owner who is much like himself.

This lively, inquisitive, gregarious dog is most content with someone who is fascinated rather than exasperated by canine curiosity, who gladly returns a dog's affection and attention, who enjoys abundant amounts of routine physical activity and who is willing to understand and accept a dog for what that dog is meant to be. Living up to such a dog's expectations can be a rewarding experience.

Misconceptions About the Husky

The most common misconception about Siberian Huskies and, frankly, most of their Nordic cousins, is they have no sense and no intelligence. To label the breed so indicates that the speaker knows nothing about Siberians.

Just what is canine intelligence? Is it a willingness to obey every human command without question? The Siberian doesn't think so, and he conveys his opinion on this most brazenly each day. No, to the Siberian and to those who love him, the intelligent dog is the one who decides for himself, according to his own thoughts at the moment, whether he will obey. In short, the Siberian may entertain a command, but he will obey only if he deems that to do so is relevant.

Such behavior is actually an ancient gift of survival to the human species, most clearly illustrated by the Siberian Husky's sled dog heritage. In both historic and current times, the Siberian has been entrusted with his musher's life. When that musher commands the lead dog to go right, but the dog knows through his superior canine senses

A DOG'S SENSES

Sight: With their eyes located farther apart than ours, dogs can detect movement at a greater distance than we can, but they can't see as well up close. They can also see better in less light, but can't distinguish many colors

Sound: Dogs can hear about four times better than we can, and they can hear high-pitched sounds especially well. Their ancestors, the wolves, howled to let other wolves know where they were; our dogs do the same, but they have a wider range of vocalizations, including barks, whimpers, moans and whines.

Smell: A dog's nose is his greatest sensory organ. His sense of smell is so great he can follow a trail that's weeks old, detect odors diluted to one-millionth the concentration we'd need to notice them, even sniff out a person under water!

Taste: Dogs have fewer taste buds than we do, so they're likelier to try anything—and usually do, which is why it's especially important for their owners to monitor their food intake. Dogs are omnivores, which means they eat meat as well as vegetable matter like grasses and weeds.

Touch: Dogs are social animals and love to be petted, groomed and played with.

that to go right means death, the dog follows his own instincts and disobeys. The savvy musher recognizes the dog's instincts and can't help but be grateful.

Of course such a potentially headstrong dog is not what every dog owner looks for in a pet. Yet for those who do, there is nothing more stunning than the Siberian's mind at work—and nothing more challenging.

We see the Siberian Husky's mind at work in the speed with which he will take advantage of a situation if afforded the chance. We see it in the selective hearing that so many Siberians have mastered when faced with commands they'd rather ignore. We see it in the ingenuity they employ when the inspiration strikes them to create a new game. Success in dealing with such an independent thinker thus requires an owner who can stay one step ahead of the dog—and keep life interesting for the Siberian at the same time.

The Husky's headstrong nature is a result of breeding for a dog who could make his own decisions on the trail.

Are You Up to the Challenge?

Tragically, far too many of these beautiful, affectionate dogs wind up in animal shelters and with breed rescue groups each year, invariably the victims of misunderstandings between dogs and their owners. Perhaps their owners weren't up to the challenge of working with such dogs. Perhaps they didn't have the time. Or perhaps they simply didn't make the effort to learn more about the animal with which they were dealing.

The very pack-oriented Siberian Husky is extremely sensitive to family pecking orders, and if one of the human members doesn't accept the role of family pack leader (or alpha), your Siberian will gladly step in and accept it. Convincing your dog otherwise must not be a test of physical prowess or force but rather a show that you understand your Siberian's view of the world and respect him for it, but expect him in turn to respect you as lead dog.

Consistency lies at the heart of establishing this pack relationship. Your dog must learn quickly what behavior is and is not acceptable. If he is caught in the midst of an unacceptable act, such as chewing on Dad's shoes, he must be corrected with firm yet gentle discipline at that moment and every time he indulges in that act in the future (of course, your dog should not be given shoes to chew on as toys, either). Basic training and behavior problem corrections must be pursued with positive reinforcement, which shows your dog how rewarding his compliance with acceptable behavior expectations can be.

It is imperative to teach your Husky what is and is not expected of him. With positive reinforcement, you can do anything with him.

Train to Gain

Seeking professional help is also a positive step toward teaching your Siberian what is expected of him and in forging the bond between the dog and his family. Obedience classes, for example, offer the ideal opportunity for both teaching and socializing dogs, and they prove invaluable in training owners as well. Be warned, however, that proper screening of potential trainers is imperative. Many professional dog trainers will readily confess that Nordic breeds can be a challenge to train—perhaps even a challenge that exceeds their own skills. But just as there are plenty of ideal Siberian Husky owners out there, so are there dog trainers who relish the opportunity to work with this breed.

The properly prepared owner and trainer understands that Siberians are quick learners, yet the dogs become easily and quickly bored, especially with training that involves endless repetition.

The Siberian Husky is born to run, and thrives when he is given the opportunity to do so.

Make It a Game

Veterans of Siberian training suggest that training sessions be limited to only about fifteen minutes a shot and that the trainer be creative in his or her techniques. Make training a game. Feed into your Siberian's naturally inquisitive nature, perhaps with hide-and-seek games or by alternating command training with play with a favorite toy.

Training, whether done officially with a professional or at home with the family, should be done with specific goals in mind. Training your Siberian, a dog with a natural inclination to pull, to heel, for example, can be difficult. Unless your dog is destined for the obedience or conformation showring, perhaps just teaching him the basics—not to pull on the leash, the sit command and the down—is enough. Defining the training goals will help ensure success for all parties. (For more on training see Chapter 8.)

Born to Run

Warning: NEVER allow your Siberian Husky to run loose!

In lists of instructions to new owners on the nuances of Siberian ownership, this statement is invariably the most important. Genetically programmed to run, your Siberian Husky will do so whenever he is offered the opportunity.

Siberians are obsessed with running. A hole in the fence, a slipped collar, a faint sound in a distant neighborhood, and your Siberian will answer that ancient genetic call within his soul and run, not because he is unhappy in his current surroundings, but because he simply must. He has no choice.

Though the running is genetic, nature has not provided the Siberian with an equally powerful homing instinct. The consequences, then, are clear. When your dog finally stops running, he will look around, probably not even realize he is lost and happily follow the first person he sees meandering by, even one who may mean harm.

Huskies love to chew and dig, and they need plenty of exercise.

Reining In a Wanderer

If this wandering Siberian is lucky, the person who finds the dog will be one willing to help the animal get home. If he's even luckier, the dog's owner

will have prepared for just such an event by outfitting him with current identification tags or perhaps other more high-tech means of ID such as a registered tattoo on the groin or a microchip beneath the skin. Of course, there's always the danger that whoever finds this friendly, breathtakingly beautiful beast may just not want to give him back.

With the Siberian's natural inclination to wander—a habit that can lead to injury, theft or the many dangers that face a dog who becomes a neighborhood nuisance—the wise owner does not allow his or her dog to get away in the first place by providing the dog with proper housing (more on that in Chapter 4), attention and supervision.

Natural Inclinations

Siberian Huskies love to **chew** (first while teething as puppies; later as a way of venting stress and excess energy), and they love to **dig** (a habit from their ancestors who would dig nests in the snow). Their need and desire to partake in these undeniably canine activities are directly related to the amount of attention and exercise they are receiving at a given time.

It's really not fair to bar your Siberian from digging and chewing entirely. Rather, it is best to accommodate your dog in a controlled manner that prevents wanton destruction of the house or yard. Doing this is simple enough: Provide your dog with plenty of sturdy chew toys to his liking (experimentation may be required to identify his favorites), and if possible, provide him with a digging place, a spot in the yard where he knows digging is allowed.

The digging place may be possible only if you have your own backyard, but there are alternatives. Winter offers ample digging opportunities if snow is on the ground, but in the summer, or in regions that get no snow, take your dog to the beach or perhaps to a river surrounded by soft earth. Here your dog can dig to his heart's content.

Exercise Is a must

The Siberian Husky, a veritable font of energy, requires **plenty of exercise** to help expend the energy he builds both in mind and body each day. This need not be

---

CHARACTERISTICS OF A SIBERIAN HUSKY

lively

curious

needs a lot of routine physical exercise

loves to run

independent-minded

devoted to family

a great deal of exercise—some fanciers suggest that a half hour a day of vigorous activity will suffice. Such a commitment will, for obvious reasons, benefit both dog and owner.

Running around in the yard alone day in and day out will not do. The Siberian's insatiable hunger for new sights and sounds must be satisfied as well as his physical needs. This is, after all, a world-class athlete bred for both endurance and adaptability to new environs.

Siberians love the attention and companionship they get from their human family, as these posers demonstrate.

Providing adequate exercise does not mean your Siberian must be mushed through the tundra to make him happy, although recreational mushing is becoming more popular every year. Daily jogging; pulling the kids on a sled or in a wagon (with proper sled dog harness!); long walks through the neighborhood or, for the truly brave, in-line skating with a Siberian in tow are all excellent activities for a Siberian Husky. Please note, however, that all these activities do involve a Siberian on a leash or in a harness—in other words, a Siberian under control.

Use your imagination in dealing with this dog. Refuse to do so and your Siberian surely will use *his* imagination, especially when it comes to dreaming up new and creative methods of destruction—all in the name of fun.

In Need of a Family

The Siberian Husky's life is family. The trouble is everyone is his family, a sentiment unappreciated by people who believe their Siberian will guard their home and hearth. Although Siberians are independent souls, their genetic code mandates an affinity for humans. They are profoundly devoted to their families—and to virtually everyone else they happen to encounter.

While the Siberian's size, wolfy appearance and otherworldly eyes may be a deterrent to would-be attackers, this is no guard dog. Watchdog? Ask breeders. Sure, he'll watch anyone who comes into the home, and then show them where to find the valuables—all with that irrepressible Siberian smile.

An Attention-Seeker

Nor do most Siberians make for good latchkey dogs. Their very social natures demand attention, and most will push their way into every family activity—and make everyone miserable if they can't do so. That desire has made the Siberian a very adaptable animal who loves to travel to new locales (with appropriate confinement and leash, of course), a longing that obviously stems from his historic travels on the ice.

Although the Siberian Husky revels in a frozen climate, he will adapt well to both rural and urban living in any region of the country. He simply asks for doses of companionship and exercise and that exercise sessions during the warmer months of the year be scheduled for the cooler hours of the day.

At the core of their adaptability is the Siberian's genuine love of family—and, especially, of children. Despite his independence, like all Nordic breeds the Siberian Husky is uncannily attuned to family relationships. For obvious reasons, he is the ideal candidate for a multidog household and, in fact, may fare best in the company of other dogs. This in turn helps keep separation anxiety—and the resultant destructive behavior and neighbor-annoying howling—at bay.

Cats, Beware!

As for other animals—particularly cats—beware. Predatory instincts natural to the breed can cause your Siberian Husky to chase and kill cats, which is why many people involved in Siberian placement, either as breeders or as part of Siberian Husky breed rescue, will not place their charges in homes with cats. All may be well if a Siberian puppy is raised with a cat, but he may subsequently as an adult grant clemency only to *that* cat, while all others remain fair game.

MORE INFORMATION ON THE SIBERIAN HUSKY

NATIONAL BREED CLUB

Siberian Husky Club of America
Mrs. Fain B. Zimmerman
65 Madeira Dr.
Victoria, TX 77905-4847

The club can give you information on all aspects of the breed, including the names and addresses of breed, obedience and sledding clubs in your area or elsewhere. Inquire about membership.

BOOKS

Brearley, Joan McDonald. *The Siberian Husky.* Neptune, NJ: TFH Publications, 1992.

Jennings, Michael. *The New Complete Siberian Husky.* New York, NY: Howell Book House, 1992.

Kern, Kerry. Siberian Huskies: *A Complete Pet Owner's Manual.* Hauppauge, NY: Barron's Educational Series, 1990.

Pisano, Beverly. *Siberian Huskies.* Neptune, NJ: TFH Publications, 1989.

VIDEOS

Siberian Huskies. The American Kennel Club.

MAGAZINES

International Siberian Husky Club News
N. 7002 Plick Station Rd.
Elkhorn, WI 53121-9417

The Siberian Husky Club of America Newsletter
Leslie Crawford, Editor
109 Weatherly Way
Pelham, AL 35124

Living

with a

part two

Siberian
Husky

chapter 4

Bringing Your
Siberian Husky
Home

Few can resist the charms of a puppy, especially a Siberian Husky puppy—a soft, roly-poly ball of fluff that looks more like a bear cub than the wolf that she will someday resemble. But within that ball of fluff lurks the heart of one of the most demanding, time-consuming little creatures anyone could ever hope to meet.

Because of the responsibilities inherent in puppy raising, many people prefer bringing an older dog into the household. What they may or may not realize, however, is that this, too, brings with it responsibilities. The moral of the story is whether you choose a puppy or an adult Siberian, one thing's for certain: That Siberian will bounce in, win the hearts of all she meets and undoubtedly take over the house.

You, in turn, would be wise to know what to expect and to be prepared with the proper supplies.

Laying the Foundation

The first year that a dog or puppy spends with her new family is an adjustment period for all involved. Although we will examine the puppy's introduction as the example, her experiences with the new home— and the family's subsequent response—can actually apply to adult dogs as well (after all, that inner puppy lives in every dog).

Regardless of your dog's age, when she arrives in the home the dynamics of the household are in for a change. Everyone will have to work to establish the new pet's place in the family and his or her own contribution to her care. This is also the ideal time to build a solid foundation that will carry the puppy or dog through her early months with her new family and into the years to come.

Puppyhood can be a trying time. Puppies require a great deal of attention as you take over mom's role in teaching your puppy how to be a civilized canine citizen. In the weeks and months to come you and your puppy will need to address basic training (which may begin with puppy kindergarten classes at three months of age), housetraining, canine manners at home and outside and your puppy's overall health and physical development.

Natural Curiosity

The young Siberian Husky is more likely to be curious about than afraid of her surroundings. That curiosity could lead her to chew electrical chords, poisonous plants or glass Christmas ornaments (especially when teething begins at about three months of age). A selection of chew toys, constant supervision and puppy proofing of the home environment (just as parents would do for a human child) could save your dog's life.

PUPPY ESSENTIALS

Your new puppy will need:

food bowl

water bowl

collar

leash

I.D. tag

bed

crate

toys

grooming supplies

Curious or not, all puppies deserve some sensitivity from their owners to the great transition they are experiencing. In all your dealings with the young animal, you must make positive reinforcement the guiding concept and accept that your puppy will make mistakes and, of course, "have accidents" while she is working to understand what is expected of her.

It is also important to provide your puppy with a comforting, confined spot in the house that is all her own—perhaps a corner in the kitchen or in some other room of the house. Here your puppy can retreat to take a nap (puppies require a great deal of sleep), and here you may confine your puppy when she is left alone in the house.

Another option many breeders recommend is a crate—a denlike accommodation in which your puppy may be confined at night and when no one is at home. A crate provides her with both security and safety. One large enough for your puppy or dog to turn around in and furnished with a soft blanket and some chew toys may quickly become your puppy's, and someday your dog's, favorite voluntary sleeping place.

Puppyhood can be a trying time as your dog adjusts to your family. Safe toys are a must.

Basic Health Concerns

Within those first few months your puppy should receive a full series of vaccines, spaced several weeks apart, which culminate with the rabies vaccine at age four months. The immunity the vaccines provide is critical for a dog that will someday be spending a great deal of time outdoors and with other dogs. (See Chapter 7 for more information.)

The vaccination appointments offer the ideal opportunity for your puppy to develop a healthy relationship with her veterinarian and to accustom your dog to examinations. The pet owner can help at home by touching the pup's ears and feet in fun and even introducing her to grooming and tooth brushing. Keep such sessions short, light and upbeat.

Now is also the time to think about spaying and neutering. The younger a dog is altered, the healthier she is likely to be and the longer she is likely to live. The altered dog's temperament also tends to be more stable because she is free from hormone-induced distractions that can lead intact animals astray and divert their attentions from their owners.

From a civic standpoint, spaying or neutering ensures that a dog will never accidentally contribute to the problem of pet overpopulation. In the case of the Siberian Husky, altering also helps preserve the quality of the breed. While most Siberians make wonderful pets, only a small percentage of the breed are of breeding quality. Breeding is best left to those who have devoted their lives and a great deal of their finances to it. Such individuals pursue this activity out of a passion for the breed—a passion that produces beautiful, affectionate pets as well as stunning show dogs.

Make sure your puppy gets all her shots on schedule to keep her healthy.

Six months has long been generally accepted as the appropriate age for spaying and neutering (for a female, spaying before the first heat cycle is ideal). Six months also happens to fall right in the heart of canine adolescence, the time from about four to ten months of age. As anyone with experience knows, during this time the dog behaves just as one would expect from an adolescent, especially when the dog in question is so headstrong an animal as the Siberian Husky.

At this stage, both the dog's appearance and behavior begin to change. Physically, your puppy will evolve almost magically from a fluffy ball of fur to a gangly adolescent with ears that are too large and legs that are too long. But in a few months that ugly duckling will blossom into the beautiful swan that is the adult Siberian Husky. Meanwhile, stick to your guns. Feeling independent and strong, the Siberian adolescent may be inclined to challenge her leader for that position and to disobey commands just out of the sheer pleasure of doing so. You must convince your young dog otherwise in a firm yet gentle manner.

Safe Housing

All dogs need to chew; all dogs need protection from household dangers; all dogs need companionship; and all dogs, especially Siberian Huskies, need fail-safe confinement outdoors.

If your dog spends a great deal of time outdoors, an enclosed, chain-link dog kennel run, preferably the type with a roof, is ideal. A backyard with a fence that stands a minimum of six feet high is nice, too, but can prove dangerous, especially if the fencing is not anchored deeply into the ground or if your dog finds a small hole beneath the fence that she can excavate for freedom, adventure and running. Never underestimate a Siberian's digging abilities—or her skills as escape artist extraordinaire.

Siberians are not known as jumpers, but they have been known to scale or climb a fence, especially from the roof of a doghouse positioned next to that fence.

HOUSEHOLD DANGERS

Curious puppies and inquisitive dogs get into trouble not because they are bad, but simply because they want to investigate the world around them. It's our job to protect our dogs from harmful substances, like the following:

IN THE HOUSE

cleaners, especially pine oil

perfumes, colognes, aftershaves

medications, vitamins

office and craft supplies

electric cords

chicken or turkey bones

chocolate

some house and garden plants, like ivy, oleander and poinsettia

IN THE GARAGE

antifreeze

garden supplies, like snail and slug bait, pesticides, fertilizers, mouse and rat poisons

And speaking of doghouses, the outdoor Siberian should have access to a well-insulated doghouse for shelter from the weather, but don't be surprised if she chooses not to use it in the snow. Many a Siberian prefers, like her ancestors, to curl up in a ball in the snow with her tail wrapped around her body in natural protection from the cold.

Puppies—and adult dogs— need a supply of collars and leashes for various activities.

Your dog may deign to use her house in the rain, but better yet, in a downpour, why not bring her inside? Yes, Siberians adore the great outdoors, but they also adore sharing the hearth of the family pack. While your dog may spend a great deal of time outdoors (preferably with companion dogs), indoors with her family is where she belongs at least part of every day, rain or shine.

chapter 5

Feeding

Your

Siberian Husky

For centuries, many viewed the Siberian Husky as a machine, even before the advent of machines as we know them. Mushers have long relied on the endurance and efficiency of Huskies on the trail, thus acknowledging, knowingly or not, just how critical food (or fuel) is to keeping that machine contented, purring and running smoothly.

For such an active dog, on the trail or in the home, only a high-quality, balanced diet can properly fuel that legendary font of energy that lies within, keeping his body healthy and his mind alert. To live up to his birthright as an energetic, fun-loving dog, an owner has no choice but to ensure that this breathtakingly beautiful machine remains ready and able to keep up with any activity that strikes his fancy.

Basic Nutrition

The Siberian Husky is the perfect combination of companion and athlete, thus requiring a diet worthy of both callings. The healthy Siberian exhibits a lustrous, thick coat and shining eyes—characteristics of beauty that appear skin deep but that rely heavily on what is going on inside. Specifically, poor nutrition leads to a deterioration of external appearances, providing us with very obvious signs of internal problems. On the other hand, proper, high-quality food helps maintain your dog's ideal.

Traditionally, Siberian Huskies were bred to survive on relatively small amounts of food—a diet that basically consisted of scraps of frozen fish or whatever other game the Chukchi hunter was fortunate enough to obtain for his family as well as for his dogs. Fortunately, feeding the modern-day Siberian is quite a bit easier.

All dogs require a balanced diet. According to the principles of basic canine nutrition, the nutrients must all be present—proteins, fats, carbohydrates, vitamins and minerals—but they must blend within a balanced formula. This formula lies at the heart of that beautiful coat, those shining eyes and those efficient internal organs.

A common misconception is that if a little is good, more must be better—not so in nutrition, canine or

> **HOW MANY MEALS A DAY?**
>
> Individual dogs vary in how much they should eat to maintain a desired body weight—not too fat, but not too thin. Puppies need several meals a day, while older dogs may need only one. Determine how much food keeps your adult dog looking and feeling her best. Then decide how many meals you want to feed with that amount. Like us, most dogs love to eat, and offering two meals a day is more enjoyable for them. If you're worried about overfeeding, make sure you measure correctly and abstain from adding tidbits to the meals.
>
> Whether you feed one or two meals, only leave your dog's food out for the amount of time it takes her to eat it—10 minutes, for example. Freefeeding (when food is available any time) and leisurely meals encourage picky eating. Don't worry if your dog doesn't finish all her dinner in the allotted time. She'll learn she should.

otherwise. The nutrients seek balance and harmony with each other for the good of the body at large. Get too little or too much of one, especially vitamins and minerals, and the other nutrients, as well as the bodily functions with which they interact, can all be sent into a tailspin.

The moral of the story? Over-nutrition can be just as dangerous as malnutrition. With one exception . . .

water. This is the nutrient a dog can almost never have enough of. Like our bodies, dogs' bodies are largely composed of water, and dehydration is a serious threat to life. Make sure your Husky always has access to a bowl of clean, cool, fresh water. Wash any water bowls thoroughly every day, especially outdoor bowls, to keep bacteria and flies at bay. The only time water should be restricted is just before bed during early puppyhood, when housetraining rules are being established.

To maintain optimum health, determine your Husky's nutritional needs and feed him one of the commercial dog foods available today.

Food Quality

Every year pet food manufacturers invest millions of dollars in research to determine what dogs should and should not be eating. In exchange for such investments, they enjoy a tidy profit—and dogs share the wealth as well.

The best diet for a dog, any dog, is simple: a high-quality commercial diet, readily available in pet supply and grocery stores. The key phrase is "high-quality." In other words, ignore the generics. Safest are those foods approved by the Association of American Feed Control Officials (noted on the packaging). This approval means the food meets the standards of what is currently accepted as best for man's best friend.

Such foods come in several forms. The simplest and most hassle-free is dry kibble, although some owners like to spice up the kibble with a touch of canned food thrown in for flavor (some owners feed half and half). With a quality product, as long as the correct amount and balance are there—and as long as the dog shines like a picture of health—all is well.

You may harbor a romantic notion of feeding your pet a home-cooked diet, but unless you have a doctorate in canine nutrition, you could endanger your dog with a diet in which nutrients are out of balance. Let those veterinarians and nutritionists at the manufacturing companies do the dirty work. Nutrition is, after all, a science.

That science can come in handy for the Siberian athlete. While most pet Siberians should do well with a basic high-quality maintenance diet, the serious racer in heavy training, for example, will require more than the pet's diet can offer.

High-energy foods are available for such dogs who may require nutritional supplements and even table scraps. But offering a pet, even a very active pet, similar cuisine probably won't mesh with his needs, and in most cases, supplements can throw the pet's diet off kilter. The

HOW TO READ THE DOG FOOD LABEL

With so many choices on the market, how can you be sure you are feeding the right food for your dog? The information is all there on the label—if you know what you're looking for.

Look for the nutritional claim right up top. Is the food "100% nutritionally complete"? If so, it's for nearly all life stages; "growth and maintenance," on the other hand, is for early development; puppy foods are marked as such, as are foods for senior dogs.

Ingredients are listed in descending order by weight. The first three or four ingredients will tell you the bulk of what the food contains. Look for the highest-quality ingredients, like meats and grains, to be among them.

The Guaranteed Analysis tells you what levels of protein, fat, fiber and moisture are in the food, in that order. While these numbers are meaningful, they won't tell you much about the quality of the food. Nutritional value is in the dry matter, not the moisture content.

In many ways, seeing is believing. If your dog has bright eyes, a shiny coat, a good appetite and a good energy level, chances are his diet's fine. Your dog's breeder and your veterinarian are good sources of advice if you're still confused.

only supplement required for every dog is a steady stream of fresh water.

Feeding for Different Life Stages

Through all that research that goes on for the formulation of dog foods, manufacturers have further narrowed the field by offering products designed to meet a dog's nutritional needs at various stages of life.

If you're feeding more than one Husky, you'll need to supervise mealtime to make sure all are getting their fair share.

Specialized products begin with **puppyhood** and the diets formulated to facilitate the accelerated growth puppies experience during their first eighteen mon ths or so.

For the slower metabolism, but high energy needs, of the **adult dog,** an adult maintenance diet should suffice. Then, when your dog reaches age seven or so, it may be wise to switch to a diet formulated for the **older dog.** Senior diets are lower in fat (for dogs who have put on a few too many pounds through the years) and protein (placing less strain on the older dog's urinary tract). There are numerous foods to choose from for all these life stages. Consult with your veterinarian or fellow Husky owners if you want advice on which is best for your dog.

Fighting Fat

Excess poundage is not the sole domain of the older dog. Owners who revel in sharing a slice of birthday cake with the family pet or allowing him to "clear" the dinner plates every night must realize that obesity is a major health risk for dogs that undermines an animal's quality and length of life.

Fortunately, it is rare to see an obese Siberian Husky. Yet breeders warn that you must take great care not to overfeed this animal, which was bred for an efficient metabolism and limited dietary needs. That extraordinary Siberian metabolism may be overwhelmed by a modern diet, and the dog could gain weight on the amounts of food prescribed on the package for that size dog.

For that rogue Siberian Husky that has succumbed to the lure of too many table scraps from his master's table, light canine diets are available. These satisfy his hunger while remaining lower in fat and calories to facilitate weight loss—assuming of course that you also commit to reducing or, preferably, eliminating treats and table scraps from your dog's menu.

> **TO SUPPLEMENT OR NOT TO SUPPLEMENT?**
>
> If you're feeding your dog a diet that's correct for her developmental stage and she's alert, healthy-looking and neither over- nor underweight, you don't need to add supplements These include table scraps as well as vitamins and minerals. In fact, a growing puppy is in danger of developing musculoskeletal disorders by oversupplementation. If you have any concerns about the nutritional quality of the food you're feeding, discuss them with your veterinarian.

How Much to Feed Your Husky

When you bring your Husky puppy home, if he's between six and ten weeks old, you can expect to feed him three or four times a day. Start your puppy on kibble, preferably the same brand he was eating before you got him. If you want to switch brands, do so gradually, mixing small amounts of the new food in with the old until all the old is replaced with the new.

The person from whom you got your puppy can probably recommend how much to feed him at each meal, and you can ask your veterinarian when you take your pup in for his examination and vaccines. Mix the kibble with some warm water and let it soften some before feeding.

At around twelve weeks of age you can cut back to three meals a day, reducing to two when your pup's six months or older.

There is no set serving amount ideal for every Siberian. For the adult, depending on your individual dog and his calling, he may require anywhere from two to four cups of dry food a day. Your veterinarian can help determine the ideal for your dog, assisted of course by your knowledge of your pet.

About Treats

Treats can be a downfall for many a dog, but for the animal who isn't overweight, they are a delight—and an effective training tool. Stick to treats made for dogs and ones that complement an intelligent nutrition plan.

The best rule is to avoid "people food" altogether (especially chocolate, which is poisonous to dogs). Yes, it's tempting to fall prey to those pleading eyes asking for just a little bit of lo mein or spaghetti, but to reward that or any other begging behavior is to encourage it from then on—and to foster an unhealthy dog. So dump the table scraps, or keep them for leftovers. Your dog is not a garbage disposal.

TYPES OF FOODS/TREATS

There are three types of commercially available dog food—dry, canned and semimoist—and a huge assortment of treats (lucky dogs!) to feed your dog. Which should you choose?

Dry and canned foods contain similar ingredients. The primary difference between them is their moisture content. The moisture is not just water. It's blood and broth, too, the very things that dogs adore. So while canned food is more palatable, dry food is more economical, convenient and effective in controlling tartar buildup. Most owners feed a 25% canned/75% dry diet to give their dogs the benefit of both. Just be sure your dog is getting the nutrition he needs (you and your veterinarian can determine this).

Semimoist foods have the flavor dogs love and the convenience owners want. However, they tend to contain excessive amounts of artificial colors and preservatives.

Dog treats come in every size, shape and flavor imaginable, from organic cookies shaped like postmen to beefy chew sticks. Dogs seem to love them all, so enjoy the variety. Just be sure not to overindulge your dog. Factor treats into her regular meal sizes.

Keep Track of What You Feed

Feeding methods are also something to think about. Some dogs can be free fed, meaning dry food may be left for them at all times, allowing them to nibble whenever they feel a pang. This is not a recommended feeding style, however, for several reasons. First is health. One of the earliest signs that your dog may not be feeling well is a loss of appetite. A healthy Husky should be eager for mealtime. If you free-feed your dog and he doesn't go for the food right away, you may not suspect his appetite is off until the end of the day when you see no food was eaten. Another reason not to free-feed has to do with behavior. As the meal provider for your dog, you gain elevated status and control. Free-feed, and your dog doesn't *need* you to have its appetite sated.

Along these lines, you shouldn't even be too generous with scheduled mealtimes. If your dog doesn't finish his food within fifteen minutes of putting the bowl down, pick the bowl up and don't feed him again until the next mealtime. Healthy Huskies have healthy appetites and should have no problem finishing meals.

If you feed several dogs together (not unusual in a Siberian Husky home), you must carefully observe the scene at feeding time to ensure that all are getting their fair share. A more aggressive dog may keep a submissive counterpart away from the food. If this occurs, feed the dogs in separate locations.

Dogs may also exhibit preferences for certain foods. That's fine, but once one works, stick with it. Variety need not be an issue. Owners should have a say in the choice of these products because the results intimately involve them.

Canned foods, for example, contain more moisture than do dry: Your dog must therefore eat more and, in the end, eliminate more. Your dog may be able to eat less of the more expensive, so-called premium dry foods, resulting in an end by-product that is firm, compact and easier to clean up.

The End Result

Which brings us to the unfortunate fact that no discussion of canine nutrition is complete without talk of the digestive system's by-products. Feces, in fact, offer a valuable tool for evaluating a dog's health. Any unusual changes in consistency color and so forth could indicate illness within. Your dog should defecate daily, and you should check for changes daily as well.

To prevent those telltale changes and to prevent diarrhea and nausea, keep the diet steady. Make no sudden changes. If alterations must be made, do so gradually, mixing the old food with the new food over several days to help the digestive system adjust.

Although Siberians don't necessarily eat as much as we would expect from dogs their size, they may eat more in winter than in summer to fuel their energy needs for winter sports and to help maintain body heat.

Water, too, is just as critical in winter, yet many dogs refuse to drink sufficiently in the cold. Take a tip from many an Iditarod racer—spike the water with meat broth or some other irresistible flavoring. Your dog will willingly imbibe when so bribed and thus sufficiently hydrate his body. Make sure, too, to change the water in an outdoor dish frequently during the day in freezing temperatures to prevent the water from icing up.

chapter 6

Grooming
Your
Siberian Husky

One fact Siberian Husky owers must face very early in their relationship with this dog is that when walking down the street with a Siberian in tow, it's the dog that will receive most of the attention from onlookers. This attention should cause no animosity nor come as a surprise because the dog's great beauty is why most people find themselves attracted to this breed in the first place.

To maintain that beauty, a surprisingly minimal amount of effort is required. Breeding their dogs in the snow for hard work, the Chukchis could not afford a coat that demanded a great deal of care. Their commonsense selective breeding has resulted in an easy-care

animal that with just a bit of routine attention will
remain a sparkling example of canine beauty.

A Double-Coated Dog

There is nothing more eye-catching than the well-
groomed Siberian. Good grooming involves understanding the unique properties of the breed's coat.

*The Husky's
unique coat
helps keep her
warm in winter
and cool in
summer.*

The Siberian's double coat—the soft, dense, fluffy
undercoat protected by longer guard hairs—works to
warm the dog in the subzero temperatures from which
the breed hails. As an added benefit, the body's own
self-maintenance of this coat is as inspiring as the effi-
ciency with which the coat functions.

While the Siberian sheds as any other dog of its coat
length does, once or twice a year most experience an
unusually heavy shed, referred to as "blowing coat."
Over several weeks, the undercoat comes out in great,
soft handfuls. The prepared caretaker in turn stands
ready with comb and brush to keep the process under
control.

Despite how lovely the Siberian may look in full coat,
when it comes time to blow, you must resist the
impulse to brush your dog only superficially, bypassing
the skin and therefore retaining the appearance of a
full coat. Without proper grooming (more like har-
vesting) during this time, those loose hairs will become

trapped next to the skin, retaining moisture and heat that can lead to skin problems, especially in warmer temperatures.

This is not to suggest that in the summer's heat, the Siberian Husky should be shaved. On the contrary, your dog's unique coat works just as effectively to keep her cool as it does to keep her warm; to remove that natural protection by shaving is to expose the skin to elements it was never meant to see.

A clean, dry, freshly bathed Husky—or three—makes for a pretty picture.

Routine Brushing

Your role in maintaining the health of your Siberian Husky's skin and coat is relatively simple.

Short yet thorough brushing sessions several times a week will prevent a monumental job later when the coat begins to blow, and it will keep shedding under control in the meantime. Brushing distributes the natural oils of the skin and coat to keep both healthy and lovely to look at, and to dogs who have been trained to sit and relax for grooming (preferably at a young age), it feels good, too.

The Siberian, like most of the Nordic breeds, doesn't usually carry the traditional doggy odor common to the species. All in all, the Siberian is a very clean breed. Routine brushing helps maintain that cleanliness by removing the dirt, plant materials and even bugs that hitch a ride in a Siberian's coat during a normal, active day. Such sessions also offer you a chance to examine your dog for lumps or bumps on the skin or anything unusual that may signal a developing health problem.

Grooming Tools

Opinions on what tools are best suited for the grooming of the Siberian's coat are as varied as the people who live and work with these dogs. For example, some veteran breeders and groomers suggest running a wide-toothed comb through the coat to remove loose hairs and undercoat, followed by a brushing with a natural bristle brush to distribute natural oils. Others, fearing that the comb pulls too much at the skin, may use a comb for loosening the undercoat but rely most heavily on the ever-popular slicker brush (for removing loose hairs) and a metal pin brush (for smoothing the coat).

**GROOMING
TOOLS**

pin brush

slicker brush

flea comb

towel

mat rake

grooming
glove

scissors

nail
clippers

tooth-
cleaning
equipment

shampoo

conditioner

clippers

Which tools you decide on is really based on what you are most comfortable using. It is on your shoulders, after all, that the grooming responsibility falls. The only rule is that your dog be brushed or combed down to the skin. There's no point and no benefit to doing a superficial job.

The comb or brush should glide easily through the Siberian's coat, for this is a breed not generally prone to matting. Mats can develop from the soft hair at the base of the ears, in the armpit or on the groin, yet routine grooming should help prevent this. Should mats develop, however, they must be removed to prevent skin rashes or infections (working them out or attempting detangling can be extremely painful to your dog). Loose mats that are far enough away from the skin can be cut out with blunt-tipped scissors; those close to the skin are best removed by a professional groomer with clippers to prevent injury.

Bathing your Husky

Because the Siberian Husky is naturally a clean breed, unless she is a show dog—and as long as she stays clear of skunks and pungent bodies of water—your dog will rarely need bathing. A few times a year will probably suffice.

Bathing may be done by turning your dog over to a capable groomer, or you can do it at home. Should you choose the latter tact, the following steps offer some basic guidelines.

First, gather the supplies. In addition to several clean towels and perhaps a washcloth and plastic rinsing cup, you will need appropriate shampoo. This should be one formulated specifically for dogs (or for puppies if your dog is a youngster). Flea shampoos help during flea season, but remember that most do not provide residual protection, so shampooing must be followed with a flea dip or spray to protect the dog postbath. Use these products only as directed to prevent toxic reactions.

Some pet owners bathe their dogs in the bathtub, whereas others prefer using a garden hose outdoors on hot summer days (with a properly restrained dog). A clean plastic garbage can or ice tub filled with water can also act as effective outdoor bathtubs. Regardless of the bathtub style used, lukewarm water reaps the greatest results and elicits the least resistance from the dog.

The Siberian is a naturally clean dog who needs a bath only occasionally.

The actual bathing process begins with a thorough brushing to remove loose hairs that may mat up once the coat is wet. At this point, some groomers place cotton in the ears and mineral oil in the eyes for protection. If you don't wish to do this, you must take great care to keep water out of the ears and soap out of the eyes.

Next, wet the coat. It may prove difficult to saturate, but keep at it. The coat must be wet to the skin, after which it's time to apply the shampoo. Scrub your dog gently from head to toe (leaving the head and face for last often makes the ordeal more bearable for some dogs). Work the shampoo down to the skin and into every nook and cranny, from between the toes to the genital and anal areas.

Once you are convinced your dog has been thoroughly cleansed, begin rinsing. Rinse and rinse and rinse, and when it appears that no more suds or bubbles are falling from the body, rinse again. Shampoo left on the coat or skin can dry out both and cause itching. With a coat as thick as the Siberian's, the rinsing process can at times seem endless.

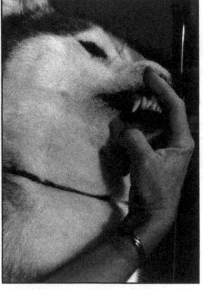

Regular brushing and professional cleaning will keep your Husky's teeth pearly white.

Dry Thoroughly

Once the coat is clean, drying begins. After an initial towel drying, try blow-drying the coat for a few minutes (on warm, not hot). After that, air-drying can finish the job. The key here is to keep your dog indoors or similarly sheltered where she will not be exposed to cold or wind until she is completely dry, undercoat and outercoat. Reaching that point can literally take all day.

When her coat is dry or almost so, brush her again. This will remove those hairs inevitably loosened by the bath. From then on, routine grooming maintenance of the coat as well as of the nails, ears and teeth will help foster the beauty that is this breed's trademark.

Caring for Nails, Ears and Teeth

Not all pet owners are comfortable trimming their dogs' nails, and not all dogs have been properly trained to accept it. Whether you tackle the job or turn it over to a groomer or veterinarian, the nails must be trimmed regularly: They are too long if they click on the ground when your dog walks.

Pay special attention to the dewclaws, the thumblike toenails higher on the foot. The dewclaws are removed from many newborn puppies, but when they are not, they can grow long and cut into the skin if not trimmed regularly.

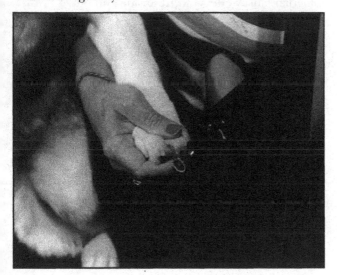

If you want, you can use a grinder after trimming your dog's nails to give them a smooth finish.

To trim the nails, use clippers designed for larger dogs. Clip the tips to avoid the quick, the usually darker, blood-rich area at the base of the nail. Nick the quick and your dog will bleed and probably not be so amenable to nail trimming the next time because of the pain "quicking" causes. Keep a styptic pencil available just in case.

Because the design of the Siberian's ears allows for proper air circulation, **ear cleaning** is relatively painless. Several swaps on the inner side of the ear flap with cotton balls or a damp washcloth should do it. (Never stick anything into the ear canal.)

Teeth, too, benefit from routine attention, meaning a **professional cleaning** twice a year by the veterinarian, and **toothbrushing** at home with a toothbrush and toothpaste made for dogs several times a week.

Convincing your Siberian to comply with such seemingly odd practices as toothbrushing and nail clipping
should begin as soon as possible in the pet and owner
relationship. Keep the sessions short (try clipping only
three or four nails per session, for example), reward
your dog with a treat at the end of each grooming
activity and keep things upbeat and positive. Such
efforts, coupled with a healthy diet, will keep your
Siberian Husky effervescent, inside and out.

chapter 7

Keeping Your
Siberian Husky
Healthy

For thousands of years the Siberian Husky had to be healthy—period. It was a matter of life and death, a matter of survival of the fittest. Today, the quest for that ideal continues with breeders understanding, as the Chukchis did, that health has everything to do with breeding.

This is not to say that such commitments, both ancient and contemporary, have instilled the Siberian with a natural immunity to health trouble. Although genetically the breed is not typically a candidate for hip dysplasia, a common canine hereditary condition, hereditary eye problems are not unusual. To combat each of these problems and to ensure they do not reach epidemic proportions, breeders urge that Siberian Huskies allowed to breed not only meet the stringent quality of their breed Standard, but also be certified free of both hip dysplasia and eye problems (more on this later).

General Health Concerns

Aside from genetic conditions, the Siberian is just as prone to the more typical canine health problems as any other dog—even more prone, in fact, to such conditions as cut paws, leg injuries, embedded foxtails, poisoning and other conditions related to the Siberian's active outdoor lifestyle. With this in mind, you must accept a great deal of responsibility in detecting potential problems as early as possible (the sooner treatment begins, the better the prognosis). You must then be prepared to clearly communicate those findings to your veterinarian.

To keep your Siberian Husky healthy for years to come, practice preventive medicine—like regular grooming, feeding a proper diet and paying attention to anything unusual.

Dogs employ a variety of techniques for letting their owners know they are not feeling up to par. Some are stoic, some hide, some want their families intimately involved. Beyond that, there are some basic signs of illness common to all dogs that tell the observant owner that veterinary attention may be in order.

Signs of Sickness

An unexplainable loss of appetite; diarrhea (especially diarrhea tinged with blood or mucus); abnormal discharges from the eyes, ears, nose or genital areas; depressed or listless behavior; lumps or bumps on the skin; poor coat quality; any unusual behavior changes; excessive thirst and urination (or strained urination) and limping are at the head of the list of symptoms that could indicate something as simple as an upset stomach or as serious as a failing internal organ. The better you, your dog's first line of defense, know your pet when he is healthy, the quicker you will recognize that something is wrong and seek treatment.

The following is a brief (and far from complete) primer on conditions that can affect Siberian Huskies. Supplement this knowledge with routine visits to your veterinarian at least once a year (more frequently as your dog ages), practice commonsense preventive health measures and call your veterinarian at the first hint of trouble and your dog will live the healthiest, most fulfilling life possible.

Preventive Medicine

OWNER VIGILENCE

As a dog owner, you are honor bound to care for and supervise your pet with responsibility and vigilance. Only this way can you detect any developing changes in health or behavior and prevent the dog from such serious health threats as, among others, dog fights, speeding cars or potential poisons. Such common-sense measures as supervision and proper confinement will keep a dog healthier and living longer, too.

ROUTINE CARE

Prevention is always the best medicine, and nowhere is this more evident than in the vision of the healthy dog. For obvious reasons, your veterinarian plays a key role here, thanks to his or her expertise in caring for patients who cannot communicate verbally about their health.

Your veterinarian is a valuable resource, but your part of the bargain is to bring your dog in at least once a year for a routine physical exam, booster vaccines, fecal exams and any other pertinent tests. Such a commitment makes life easier for both veterinarian and dog should a serious health condition be detected that will be more easily remedied with early treatment. Together, owner and veterinarian can provide the routine medical care and observation required to ensure your dog gets what he needs for optimum quality of life throughout his life.

SPAYING AND NEUTERING

Spaying or neutering a pet dog, preferably in puppyhood, is one of the most responsible steps any pet owner can take. Because only a small percentage of Siberian Huskies, or of any breed, are of breeding quality, the rest are best altered and left to live as happy, healthy family companions—made even happier and healthier because of the benefits of spaying and neutering.

Despite anthropomorphic thoughts and myths about the effects of spaying and neutering on dogs, the facts remain that altering a dog enhances health and longevity. For example, the spayed female is less prone to mammary cancer and life-threatening breeding-related illnesses, and neutered males are less prone to anal tumors and prostate problems. But the procedures reap emotional benefits as well for both the dog and his owner.

Altered dogs, unencumbered as they are by the dictates of their hormones, are more focused on their bonds with their families than are their intact

---

ADVANTAGES OF SPAY/NEUTER

The greatest advantage of spaying (for females) or neutering (for males) your dog is that you are guaranteed your dog will not produce puppies. There are too many puppies already available for too few homes. There are other advantages as well.

ADVANTAGES OF SPAYING

No messy heats.

No "suitors" howling at your windows or waiting in your yard.

Decreased incidences of pyometra (disease of the uterus) and breast cancer.

ADVANTAGES OF NEUTERING

Lessens male aggressive and territorial behaviors, but doesn't affect the dog's personality. Behaviors are often owner-induced, so neutering is not the only answer, but it is a good start.

Prevents the need to roam in search of bitches in season.

Decreased incidences of urogenital diseases.

counterparts, and they are therefore more inclined to remain contentedly at home. Their existence will also do no harm to others of their species, for they will never contribute to the tragic problem of pet overpopulation that plagues communities nationwide.

VACCINATIONS

A fundamental tenet of dog care is that dogs should be vaccinated every year. Nowhere is there a more eloquent method for fending off illness and saving hundreds of dollars in vet bills. Given that many people live with more than one Siberian Husky, current vaccines and the immunity they provide will help ensure that all within the household remain safe from communicable disease.

The dog's lifetime of vaccinations should begin during puppyhood. In his first weeks of life, the nursing puppy is protected by his mother's antibodies, but between six to eight weeks of age, he must begin to develop his own immunity. This is facilitated by vaccines for canine **distemper, hepatitis, leptospirosis, parainfluenza, parvovirus** and **coronavirus**, all administered within a single **DHLPPC vaccine**. This vaccine must be repeated every few weeks for the next few months to help ensure effectiveness after the maternal antibodies within the puppy's system begin to subside.

Those maternal antibodies can present a serious problem, for though they protect a young puppy, they work to render vaccines useless, and thus void any vaccine immunity the puppy may be developing. A conservative vaccination schedule therefore begins with the first vaccine at age six to eight weeks, followed by three more vaccines spaced about three weeks apart until the puppy reaches four months of age (the coronavirus vaccine may require only a series of two vaccines).

Veterinarians' opinions on vaccine scheduling vary widely, and research into the subject is ongoing. As more is learned about parvovirus, for example, some veterinarians are recommending that this particular vaccine, because it must combat some extraordinarily long-lived maternal antibodies within the puppy's system, be repeated up until the puppy reaches twenty or even twenty-four weeks of age. Anyone who has suffered with a puppy afflicted with this disease would not hesitate to do so.

Regardless of the original vaccine schedule you choose, your puppy should receive a DHLPPC booster at age one, setting an annual pattern to be followed for the rest of his life. Another pattern is set by the all-important rabies vaccine, without which most communities will not allow a dog to be licensed. At four months, your puppy should be vaccinated against rabies, boosters for which must follow every year or every three years thereafter, depending on the particular vaccine.

Optional vaccines include those for Lyme disease (a relatively controversial vaccine, which may or may not be necessary for dogs) and bordatella, or kennel cough (for dogs that are boarded at boarding kennels or frequently come into close contact with other dogs, particularly at dog shows).

The Eyes

Cataracts   This condition of the lens usually appears as a milky whitish or bluish cloudiness beneath the sur-

Squeeze eye ointment into the lower lid.

face of the eye. While "senile" cataracts are common in older dogs as a natural part of aging, as are cataracts in diabetic dogs, hereditary cataracts, often called juvenile cataracts, which affect younger dogs (usually before the age five), are all too com-

mon in Siberian Huskies. Some cataracts may not substantially interfere with the dog's quality of life, but if the condition severely impairs the dog's vision, the cataracts may be removed surgically.

As with progressive retinal atrophy, another genetic eye condition common to Siberians, dogs with hereditary cataracts or from lines in which the condition appears should not be bred.

Conjunctivitis Although a slight eye discharge may be normal in the healthy Siberian Husky, a profuse, often discolored discharge, red, swollen eyelid tissues and itchiness are the classic signs of conjunctivitis, an often contagious inflammation of the lining of the eyelids. Conjunctivitis is usually caused by an allergic reaction to pollens, a bacterial infection, a structural defect in the eyelids or other illnesses (as a secondary infection).

Dogs that actively participate in outdoor activities, a group from which the Siberian Husky proudly hails, can also develop conjunctivitis from foreign objects such as seeds and other plant materials that become embedded in the eye. Conjunctivitis, though rarely serious and fairly easy to treat, can be very irritating to your dog and should receive veterinary attention.

Progressive Retinal Atrophy This is a condition in which, at five to seven years of age, the cells in the retina at the back of the dog's eye begin to degenerate. You will probably first notice signs of night blindness in your dog, which gradually leads to a complete loss of his sight. Prevention is the only "treatment." Because it is a hereditary disease, only Huskies that are certified free of eye problems by the Canine Eye Registration Foundation (CERF) should be chosen to carry on their lines.

> ## YOUR PUPPY'S VACCINES
>
> Vaccines are given to prevent your dog from getting an infectious disease like canine distemper or rabies. Vaccines are the ultimate preventive medicine: They're given before your dog ever gets the disease so as to protect him from the disease. That's why it is necessary for your dog to be vaccinated routinely. Puppy vaccines start at eight weeks of age for the five-in-one DHLPP vaccine and are given every three to four weeks until the puppy is sixteen months old. Your veterinarian will put your puppy on a proper schedule and will remind you when to bring in your dog for shots.

The Ears

Maintenance The structure of the Siberian Husky's ear makes it relatively trouble-free for owners to care for. Nevertheless, the ears require routine monitoring, including weekly ear checks in which the owner examines the ears by sight and smell. It only takes a moment: Look inside for evidence of excessive brownish waxy buildup or discharge, then take a whiff. An unpleasant odor is often the first sign of ear problems. Once familiar with the scent of a healthy ear, one can more easily identify trouble should an infection begin to develop.

Professional Treatment Even though the Siberian Husky is blessed with an ear design that allows for air circulation within the ear and thus generally healthy ears, it is not unusual for any dog to develop a waxy buildup or infection in the ear canal. If your dog shakes his head incessantly or scratches his ears more than usual, he is trying to tell you that something is amiss.

Check your dog's teeth frequently and brush them regularly.

Treatments for wax buildup and infections are available from veterinarians and should be used only as directed. Most of these ointments and drops are

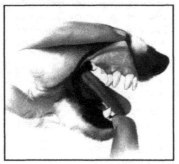

applied into the ear canal and massaged in (a process that may not thrill the patient), where they may then either fight infection or loosen excess wax. Such treatment can try the patience of any owner because the convoluted nooks and crannies of the ear canal mean that treatment may have to last several weeks to ensure success.

The Teeth

Your Husky puppy should have white, pearly teeth. So should your adult, but that isn't usually the case. Dogs, like people, are prone to the effects of poor dental hygiene—tartar and plaque buildup that leads to gingivitis, which leads to painful chewing and teeth that need to be pulled out.

Dental care is one of those areas where an ounce of prevention is worth a pound of cure. By **inspecting** and

brushing your dog's teeth regularly and getting a thorough **professional cleaning** from the veterinarian annually, your Husky should have pearly teeth all his life—and a lifetime of chewing.

Brushing your dog's teeth is easier than it sounds. The toughest part is getting him used to you handling his mouth. The best way to do that is to work slowly—first lifting his gums for a few seconds while praising him, then lifting his gums, feeling his teeth, etc. When you and he are ready, use doggy toothpaste (*never human toothpaste*) or baking soda and a bit of water on a doggy toothbrush or a finger brush or on a gauze pad. Work the brush or pad around the teeth at the gum line, just like you do with your own teeth. Dogs like the taste of the doggy paste, and shouldn't mind the baking soda. That's it! No need to rinse.

The Feet

If you can hear your Husky's toenails clicking on a hard surface, his nails are too long and need to be clipped.

To clip your Husky's nails you'll need a sturdy pair of canine nail clippers, available in a pet supply store. The ones with a safety plate so you don't cut too much off are reassuring to use. What you want to avoid is clipping into the "quick" of the toenail—a fleshy part that grows inside the nail. You'll know if you hit it because your dog will pull back in pain and the nail may bleed. Apply a styptic powder or piece of soap to the wound. It will heal, but your dog may not forgive you. That's why it's best to work carefully and consistently to make nail clipping a routine and painless procedure that neither of you dread.

WHEN TO CALL THE VET

In any emergency situation, you should call your veterinarian immediately. You can make the difference in your dog's life by staying as calm as possible when you call and by giving the doctor or the assistant as much information as possible before you leave for the clinic. That way, the vet will be able to take immediate, specific action to remedy your dog's situation.

Emergencies include acute abdominal pain, suspected poisoning, snake bit, burns, frost bite, shock, dehydration, shock, abnormal vomiting or bleeding and deep wounds.

You are the best judge of your dog's health, as you live with and observe him every day. Don't hesitate to call your veterinarian if you suspect trouble.

If your dog won't let you handle his feet, don't force him or punish him too strictly. Call a groomer or a friend with a dog and either get help holding your dog or pay a groomer to clip his nails. If left unclipped, nails can grow to curl back under the toe. They can also cause the foot to splay, which can cause other skeletal and growth abnormalities.

The Hips

Hip Dysplasia   Hip dysplasia is an abnormality in the structure of the hip joint that strikes fear in the hearts of dog owners who suddenly notice their dogs beginning to go lame in the hind legs.

Fortunately, Siberian Huskies aren't prone to hip dysplasia.

While virtually no dog is immune, the Siberian Husky is not generally prone to the disease, yet ethical breeders breed only dogs certified clear by the Orthopedic Foundation for Animals (OFA).

The OFA evaluates dogs whose hips are x-rayed at age two, and ethical breeders urge that no affected dogs or their offspring be bred. Such diligence has obviously proven effective. According to the OFA, from January 1974 to December 1994, the OFA evaluated ten thousand Siberian Huskies and found the incidence of hip dysplasia to be less than three percent.

Hip dysplasia may manifest as either a mild or severe case, usually making itself known when an owner notices a dog (often at a very early age) exhibiting an awkward gait and perhaps signs of pain. The condition will generally progress as the joint degenerates, thus causing increased pain and discomfort, further complicated if arthritis sets in.

In mild cases of hip dysplasia, pain killers prescribed by your veterinarian as well as mild exercise to retain muscle tone may be all your dog needs to enjoy life again. But in other, obviously more severe cases, major surgery, of which there are several techniques, may be the only answer and even that can be an uncertain one.

Pests and Parasites

FLEAS

The most frustrating and the most irritating (if not the most dangerous) of all parasites to plague the dog and, subsequently, his owner is the flea. The signs are obvious: incessant scratching and the appearance of fleas and flea "dirt" (flea excrement) on your dog's skin. In some warmer areas fleas are a scourge year-round; in others, dogs are blessed with a respite during the colder seasons, but whenever fleas are about, the battle plan is the same.

To combat fleas effectively, regularly treat your dog (with flea shampoos, dips or sprays), his environment (the house, the dog's bedding, the owner's bedding— preferably with products that kill preadult as well as adult fleas) and the yard. Only in this way can you hope to destroy invading fleas at all life stages, in all their favored nesting spots. Remember, however, that the products you

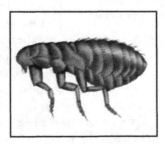

The flea is a die-hard pest.

use to combat fleas are serious insecticides. To prevent toxic reactions in your dog, choose products that are compatible with one another and with your dog, and use them only as directed.

HEARTWORM DISEASE

This parasite is extremely dangerous. Transmitted by infected mosquitoes, the preadult heartworm makes its way through your dog's bloodstream to his heart, where it grows into adulthood and works to carry on the life cycle of its species. If left untreated, heartworm will cause signs of coughing and lethargy in its victim, whom it will ultimately kill.

Treatment of heartworm disease is itself toxic, traumatic and complicated, but prevention is simple. First, an annual blood test will determine whether or not your dog has been infected. The test is then followed by the administration of effective, reasonably priced daily or monthly preventives that will help ensure your heartworm-free dog remains that way. Although heartworm is not a major problem in all regions of the nation, it has affected dogs from coast to coast, and the wise owner takes the precaution, knowing how devastating the alternative can be.

FIGHTING FLEAS

Remember, the fleas you see on your dog are only part of the problem—the smallest part! To rid your dog and home of fleas, you need to treat your dog *and* your home. Here's how:

• Identify where your pet(s) sleep. These are "hot spots."

• Clean your pets' bedding regularly by vacuuming and washing.

• Spray "hot spots" with a nontoxic, long-lasting flea larvicide.

• Treat outdoor "hot spots" with insecticide.

• Kill eggs on pets with a product containing insect growth regulators (IGRs).

• Kill fleas on pets per your veterinarian's recommendation.

INTERNAL PARASITES

Few dogs of any breed make it through a long, healthy life without experiencing an infestation of internal, usually intestinal, parasites. Roundworms, hookworms, tapeworms (transmitted by fleas), whipworms and others thrive in the innards of a dog. While such an infestation can be dangerous to young puppies, worms rarely present grave danger to adult dogs. They should, nevertheless, be eradicated swiftly.

ROUNDWORMS

These long, white worms are common internal parasites. They ocassionally infest adult dogs and people, and often infest puppies. Roundworms are transmitted via feces, when an animal walks in or eats infested feces—a good reason to pick up your dog's droppings daily and prevent your dog from investigating other dogs' feces.

If treated early, roundworms are not serious. But they must be detected and treated. Puppies with roundworms will not thrive and will appear thin but pot-bellied, with a dull coat.

HOOKWORMS

Hookworms (so called because of the hook-like teeth by which they attach themselves) live in the small intestines of dogs and suck blood from the intestinal wall. When they detach and move to a new location, the old wound continues to bleed because

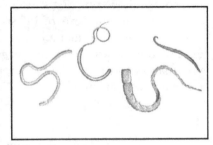

Common internal parasites (l-r): roundworm, whipworm, tapeworm and hookworm.

of the anticoagulant the worm injects when it bites. Consequently, bloody diarrhea is usually the first sign of a problem.

Like roundworms, hookworm eggs are transmitted through feces or, if conditions are right, they hatch in the soil. They then attach themselves to the feet of their new hosts, where they can burrow into the skin and migrate to the intestinal tract.

TAPEWORMS

Tapeworms also attach to the intestinal wall to absorb nutrients. As they grow they form new segments; these segments, which look like grains of rice, can be found in the dog's stools or on the area around the dog's anus if the dog is infected. The best way to prevent a tapeworm infestation is with a good flea control program, since tapeworms are acquired when a dog chews a flea bite and swallows a flea.

WHIPWORMS

Adult whipworms live in the large intestine, where they feed on blood. The eggs are passed in the dog's stool and can live in the soil for many years. A heavily infestated dog will have diarrhea that's often watery or bloody. The dog may appear thin and anemic, with a poor coat. Whipworms can be difficult to detect, as the worms do not continually shed eggs. Therefore a stool sample may be clear one day and show eggs the next.

The best ways to combat this unpleasant problem are to prevent your dog from running free and thus be exposed to various sources of worm transmission (feces of other dogs, tapeworm-carrying fleas, etc.) and to examine your dog's feces for signs of infestation. Even without signs of infestation, bring a fecal sample to your veterinarian once or twice a year for examination. If worms or their eggs are present, your veterinarian can prescribe the appropriate dewormer for that particular strain.

TICKS

Take your Siberian Husky out among the trees and vegetation, and he may just bring a tick or two home, stuck to his skin, gorging itself on his blood. Although basically harmless, ticks transmit Lyme disease and can be difficult to find on your dog's skin.

Three types of ticks (l-r): the wood tick, brown dog tick and deer tick.

Through the years many tales have circulated on how to remove ticks. The true remedy is simple: Just pull it out. On finding a tick on your dog, douse it with alcohol, then grasp its bulbous body firmly with tweezers and pull out straight, smoothly and firmly. (If tweezers are not available, use fingertips, preferably protected by a glove, a piece of plastic wrap or even a piece of paper or tissue.)

Dogs that frequently cavort in tick country, as Siberians certainly do, should be sprayed before doing so with a flea and tick spray. Your dog should then be examined carefully from head to tail at the conclusion of every romp.

Lyme Disease Should you locate and remove a tick, watch for arthritis-like signs or any other potential signs of illness for the next few weeks. These can be signals of Lyme disease, caused by a bacteria that, if diagnosed early, can be treated effectively and relatively simply with antibiotics.

The Urinary Tract

CYSTITIS

Also known as a bladder infection, cystitis occurs when bacteria infect and inflame the bladder. The affected dog will stop to urinate more fre-

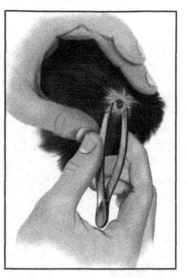

Use tweezers to remove ticks from your dog.

quently than usual, strain to urinate without much success, and perhaps break his housetraining. Also, his urine may show blood.

Any sign of urinary tract problems should be directed as soon as possible to your veterinarian, who will diagnose the condition with a urine sample. If cystitis is diagnosed, your veterinarian will prescribe antibiotics for your dog and probably ask that he be brought back in several weeks for a follow-up urinalysis to ensure the infection has been vanquished.

To help prevent cystitis, your dog should get plenty of exercise and thus ample opportunity to urinate (no drastic lifestyle change for the Siberian Husky) and drink plenty of water throughout the day to flush the bladder routinely. If this or any other urinary ailment is left untreated, it may lead to more serious problems, in this case damage to the kidneys, not to mention the discomfort it causes your dog.

KIDNEY FAILURE

The healthy kidneys clean wastes from the blood and rid the body of those wastes quickly and efficiently. If the kidneys fail, the wastes and their toxins remain in the body, and a general breakdown of organs occurs, eventually claiming the life of your dog. Various causes can lead to the development of acute

or chronic kidney failure, either of which requires immediate medical attention.

The first sign of kidney failure in dogs is usually an increase in water intake—and consequently, frequency of urination. Such observations on your part, coupled with frequent trips to your veterinarian for physical examinations and possible dietary changes to facilitate

Remember, your Husky's skin is his biggest organ, and as such is susceptible to allergies, rashes and other itch-causers.

kidney health, could keep the acute form of the disease at bay and improve the quality of your dog's life.

To protect those canine kidneys, you should offer your dog plenty of opportunities to urinate throughout the day, which will ease the stress on these vital organs. Your dog should be forbidden from running loose, a habit that could lead him to encounters with substances toxic to the kidneys such as sweet-tasting antifreeze.

STONES

In dogs, urinary stones are far more likely to form in the bladder than in the kidneys. They may form as large, often rounded, single stones or small, rough, gravellike stones, either of which can be extremely painful to your dog. They are dangerous because they block urine flow. Veterinary intervention is critical for both the health and comfort of your dog. Stones can be treated through diet, medication and, in severe cases, surgery.

The Skin

ALLERGIES

Your dog's skin, the largest organ of the body, is prone to a number of allergies, some extremely difficult to control. Although some dogs, like some humans, are allergic to pollens, grasses and food ingredients, flea saliva is a very common allergy, which can continue long after the fleas have been obliterated from both your dog and his environment.

An allergic dog will typically scratch and bite at the offending area of his body, perhaps endlessly licking his itchy feet after romping through a field of allergy-inducing grass. A dog suffering from a flea allergy is involved in a vicious cycle because his licking causes skin irritation, causing him to lick the area even more, causing even greater irritation. The site is never allowed to heal and may even develop into a related infection called pyoderma.

Allergies may be relieved with oral, topical or injectable medications prescribed by your veterinarian as well as by attempts to limit your dog's access to his allergens (some, thankfully, are seasonal). Commitment to a diligent flea control program also reaps obvious benefits.

HOT SPOTS

Hot spots—nickel-sized, red, sore and oozy patches on your dog's skin—can seem to develop overnight from no particular cause. They are deep skin infections, often caused by an insect bite or other irritation that develops into an itchy spot that the dog then licks at until it's red and raw. Your veterinarian should examine the spot to make sure it's not caused by fleas, mange or an allergy. He or she will also give you an antibiotic or topical antinflammatory medicine to treat the spot.

What's most important is that your dog can no longer itch or lick the spot. To prevent this, your vet may give you an Elizabethan collar for your dog to wear (see the illustration in this chapter).

An Elizabethan collar keeps your dog from licking a fresh wound.

MITES

These tiny parasites that thrive within the skin of your dog can cause two serious conditions that can prove difficult and time-consuming to treat: sarcoptic mange and demodectic mange.

Mites operate by burrowing into the skin, causing severe inflammation and hair loss. You may believe your dog is suffering from a generalized skin allergy only to be informed by your veterinarian after he or she examines a skin scraping of the affected area that mites are the true cause of your dog's condition. This news is never good.

An infestation of mites and the endless irritation and high contagion it brings can drive both you and your dog crazy. Your dog cannot rid himself of the discomfort, and you are faced with a rigorous treatment regimen. This may include the repeated application of medicated shampoos, dips and parasiticidal agents for weeks, antibiotics for secondary infections and vigorous treatment of the environment until the mites are gone.

TUMORS

Siberians usually are not prone to skin tumors, but you should still watch carefully for them, ideally during routine grooming sessions. Although many dogs develop fatty deposits under the skin that you feel as generic lumps and bumps, you never know when one might be a tumor.

Your veterinarian is best trained for that determination, so he or she should examine any newly discovered skin growth and biopsy it if necessary to determine whether it is malignant or benign. As with all suspected canine health problems, the earlier this diagnosis occurs, the better.

Gastrointestinal Illness

CANINE BLOAT

Technically known as gastric dilatation and torsion complex, canine bloat is an intensely painful, life-threatening condition in which gas, air and fluid build up in the dog's stomach, causing it subsequently to bloat and ultimately to twist. This acute trauma hits suddenly and violently. As it progresses, the internal turmoil squeezes the veins and arteries that transport the body's blood supply and impairs the dog's ability to breathe. Soon after the dog will die.

Bloat is a condition that requires immediate, emergency veterinary attention. Your veterinarian, by inserting a stomach tube through your dog's nose, may be able to release the gas buildup in the stomach. If at this point the stomach has twisted, no such release is possible, and surgery to untwist and anchor

IDENTIFYING YOUR DOG

It's a terrible thing to think about, but your dog could somehow, someday, get lost or stolen. How would you get him back? Your best bet would be to have some form of identification on your dog. You can choose from a collar and tags, a tattoo, a microchip or a combination of these three.

Every dog should wear a buckle collar with identification tags. They are the quickest and easiest way for a stranger to identify your dog. It's best to inscribe the tags with your name and phone number; you don't need to include your dog's name.

There are two ways to permanently identify your dog. The first is a tattoo, placed on the inside of your dog's thigh. The tattoo should be your social security number or your dog's AKC registration number.

The second is a microchip, a rice-sized pellet that's inserted under the dog's skin at the base of the neck, between the shoulder blades. When a scanner is passed over the dog, it will beep, notifying the person that the dog has a chip. The scanner will then show a code, identifying the dog. Microchips are becoming more and more popular and are certainly the wave of the future.

the stomach is the only option. To further complicate matters, the prognosis is always uncertain.

The good news is that because bloat is most common in large, deep-chested dogs, the Siberian is neither a natural nor common candidate for the condition. The bad news is that despite breed predispositions or lack thereof, bloat can happen to any dog at any time. Basic prevention, then, is imperative and not all that cumbersome.

To help prevent the conditions that can lead to bloat, feed your dog in several smaller meals a day rather than one large meal. Also schedule meals for the same times each day, do not allow your dog to exercise after a large meal, try to prevent your dog from gulping down his food (a frequent phenomenon if your dog perceives competition for his dinner from other dogs), and watch your dog carefully after he eats, so you can act quickly if you notice signs of bloat (profuse salivation, a distending abdomen, restlessness, general discomfort and unsuccessful attempts to vomit or defecate).

FOREIGN OBJECT INTESTINAL BLOCKAGE

Siberians are not typically chow hounds, but that does not mean that in their wanderings they won't be inclined to investigate and perhaps even gobble down a stick, a piece of leather, a small rubber ball or anything else that proves indigestible and unable to travel through the dogs' intestines. This item may

---

A FIRST-AID KIT

Keep a canine first-aid kit on hand for general care and emergencies. Check it periodically to make sure liquids haven't spilled or dried up, and replace medications and materials after they're used. Your kit should include:

Activated charcoal tablets

Adhesive tape
(1 and 2 inches wide)

Antibacterial ointment
(for skin and eyes)

Aspirin (buffered or enteric coated, *not* Ibuprofen)

Bandages: Gauze rolls (1 and 2 inches wide) and dressing pads

Cotton balls

Diarrhea medicine

Dosing syringe

Hydrogen peroxide (3%)

Petroleum jelly

Rectal thermometer

Rubber gloves

Rubbing alcohol

Scissors

Tourniquet

Towel

Tweezers

---

become trapped internally and cause life-threatening intestinal blockage.

The signs include vomiting, dehydration, a distended abdomen and a decidedly unhealthy fecal consistency and odor—in other words, it will present all the signs of basic gastrointestinal distress. Surgery to remove the blockage is usually the only possible treatment.

PARVOVIRUS AND CORONAVIRUS

If your dog or puppy suddenly loses his appetite, grows depressed, voids bloody diarrhea and humps his back in abdominal pain, he may be suffering from canine parvovirus or the somewhat less severe coronavirus.

Contracted through exposure to infected feces—often as innocuously as on the shoes of an owner returning home from work—these virus-induced intestinal illnesses can and frequently do kill their victims. This is especially true of puppies whose maternal antibodies have interfered with the parvo and corona vaccines they receive in their first few months of life.

Dogs who spend more time outdoors are more exposed to the elements and to other animals like skunks or porcupines. Make sure they have shade, shelter and regular attention.

While effective immunity is available through vaccination, the only cure lies within the body of the affected dog. Requiring a hospital stay, during which your veterinarian supports your dog with intravenous fluid therapy to prevent dehydration (which may claim the life of the untreated dog), it's up to your dog's

immune system to fight off the virus in the gastrointestinal tract. Whether or not the dog is successful
depends on his overall health and how fast treatment
was sought.

Outdoor Emergencies

Be Prepared It is not unusual for an active Siberian
Husky, the quintessential outdoor dog, to fall victim to
outdoor emergencies. Although it is not fair to prevent
your dog from participating in the activities he loves
best nor to prevent accidents entirely, it is possible and
even imperative to prepare for their occurrence and
know how to handle them.

Physical preparation for emergencies
means assembling a first-aid kit (for
help on what to include in the kit, see
the sidebar on page 80). So armed,
you must further prepare by learning
and understanding what dangers
might lurk out there in the great outdoors and by knowing how to act if
called on to do so.

BLEEDING WOUNDS

In the event of an injury that causes
bleeding, a safe and effective way to
stop the flow of blood is to cover the
wound with clean gauze from the
first-aid kit or any available clean

*Run your
hands regularly
over your dog
to feel for any
injuries.*

cloth and to apply direct pressure to the source of the
wound. Other methods exist, such as arterial pressure
and applying a tourniquet, but these require more
extensive training. Obviously then, it's best to obtain
such training long before ever needing to apply the
skills.

As is done in the care of wounds in humans, no matter
how minor, a dog's wound should first be cleaned thoroughly to prevent infection (this may require cutting
away some of the hair to gain access to the wound).

Next, treat the wound with antibiotic ointment, and then dress it with clean bandage materials.

Severe injuries such as puncture wounds, bites from other animals and wounds that require stitches must be treated by your veterinarian as soon as possible.

GIARDIASIS

Few can resist the allure of a cool mountain stream in the midst of a long hike in the mountains. But within that stream or any other natural body of water may lurk the protozoan that causes giardiasis.

The active Siberian Husky (or its active owner) may happily lap up the nectar from this lovely stream, only later to be plagued by persistent, often bloody, diarrhea (a sign that requires immediate veterinary attention no matter what is causing it). Some affected dogs exhibit no signs, but either way, this is a highly contagious parasitic condition that may also be transmitted through the feces of an infected dog.

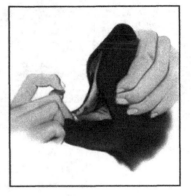

To give a pill, open the mouth wide, then drop it in the back of the throat.

Although giardiasis can be treated successfully with medication, prevention is preferable, pursued by keeping your dog's housing, feed dishes and toys sanitized; by preventing your dog from touching feces from other dogs that may be infected; and by bringing along an ample supply of your dog's own water to keep him hydrated on the trail, no matter how inviting that mountain stream might be.

PORCUPINE ENCOUNTER

Another potential drama the curious Siberian might experience is a faceful of quills from a porcupine. Although you might be inclined to giggle at this cartoonlike predicament, this situation is serious, not to mention extremely painful for your dog. Quills most commonly impale the skin on and around your dog's face, and ideally, your veterinarian should tend to their removal.

If getting your dog to your veterinarian is impossible, you will have to be the one to remove them. First, if at all possible, tranquilize and restrain your dog. Then with pliers (preferably needle-nose pliers) grasp each quill where it protrudes from the skin close to its base for good leverage, and pull the quill straight out with a smooth motion. Get your dog to your veterinarian as soon as possible; pieces of quills that have broken off can remain under the skin and cause infection.

*Make a tempo-
rary splint by
wrapping the
leg in firm
casing, then
bandaging it.*

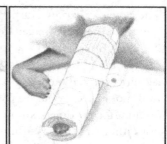

OTHER CRITTERS

Aside from porcupines, many other animals reside in the great outdoors that can easily pique the interest of the curious Siberian Husky.

If your Husky gets into a tussle with the likes of a **raccoon, groundhog, bear**—even another **dog** or a **cat**—and is bitten or scratched, treat the wound as soon as possible by cleaning it thoroughly and applying an antibiotic ointment. Of course, your dog's rabies vaccine should be current; if not, call the vet and prepare to get the vaccine updated.

If the wound is deep, get to the veterinarian as soon as possible: your dog may need stitches. If it's not that deep, clean the wound (as described), then keep a close eye on it. If it starts to ooze or look odd in any way, call the veterinarian and have it checked. Any superficial wounds should be cleaned a few times a day until properly healed.

If your Husky gets sprayed by a **skunk**, he'll be fine . . . but you'll suffer from the smell! Depending on how close your dog was when hit, you may have to throw away his collar, which could be scent-laden. A tomato-juice bath will lessen the stench, but won't get rid of it. There are commercially available "skunk-out" solutions you can try, but time is the only true cure. If possible, keep your Husky outside for several hours after the attack and limit where he can go in the house, or the smell will be everywhere.

Bites from wildlife can lead to talk of rabies, a skunk's spray could make everyone sick on the way home and a large predator could deem your Siberian a serious threat to its territory.

Help prevent such altercations and still enjoy nature with the adventure-loving Siberian Husky by resisting the urge to let your dog run loose and by keeping his rabies vaccines current.

SNAKEBITE

Most snakes the active Siberian Husky is liable to encounter in the United States are nonpoisonous, but for the unlucky dog that happens to run across a rattlesnake, copperhead, water moccasin or coral snake, the four poisonous snakes found in America, fast action is in order.

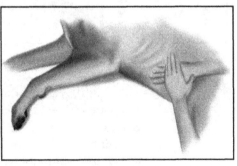

The snakes in question will leave fang marks on your dog's skin, which will swell, redden and become excruciatingly painful. Restrain your dog and keep him quiet and still to slow circulation and localize the poison. In this mode transport him to your veterinarian for treatment.

Applying abdominal thrusts can save a choking dog.

If that is not possible—say, you are out in the wilderness with your dog—the bite may be tended to with a snakebite kit. The hint here is clear: If you wander into the wilderness, buy a snakebite kit, and learn how to use it. It could prove a lifesaver for both canine and human explorers.

SHOCK

Any time a dog (or a human being) suffers a severe injury or illness that affects his blood flow and thus the heart's function, that dog is in danger of going into shock. Usually the result of severe bleeding, but also possible from acute illness, shock results from an inadequate flow of blood.

The most common cause of shock in dogs, one all too familiar to the Siberian Husky allowed to run loose, is a confrontation with a moving car. In the face of massive blood loss, the heart does all it can to get blood to the dog's vital organs, which cannot function without blood and consequently shut down. In time, if the situation is not reversed, the dog will die.

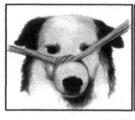

Use a scarf or old hose to make a temporary muzzle, as shown.

A dog in shock will experience a dramatic drop in body temperature and correspondingly cold extremities. He will seem dazed and disoriented and breathe rapidly. His pulse will feel fast yet weak, and his mucous membranes will pale. Your dog may be frightened, but muzzling must be done only as a last resort because it can impair your dog's already panicked attempts to breathe.

Depending on the particular case, full treatment requires not only tending to the underlying cause of shock, but also stabilizing the resulting chaos in the internal organs. In most cases, this is a job for experts.

Until you can get your dog to your veterinarian, cover him with a blanket or a jacket to help his body maintain a normal temperature; try to stop any severe bleeding; prevent him from eating or drinking; and keep him comfortable, quiet and calm (a calm owner is equally helpful). Such measures can save your dog's life in that critical time before he receives emergency veterinary treatment.

Moving your dog to transport him to treatment can also be dangerous, its success and safety depending on your dog's injury and condition. Allow him to remain in whatever position he finds most comfortable. An uncomfortable position leads to pain, which leads to stress, which leads to an acceleration of the circulatory problems that cause shock.

Your dog should be moved only as necessary: Movement may cause further injury and complicate his condition. A shock victim may fare best lying down, from which it can be moved with a large blanket or sheet folded into a hammock-style stretcher. If no such items or other hands are available for carrying your dog this way, you may have to carry him in your arms.

POISONING

Poisoning can occur from a variety of sources, anything from a pool of enticing, sweet-tasting antifreeze left in the driveway to poisonous plants your dog finds both inside and out, to cleaning solutions left in an open cabinet.

Some of the many household substances harmful to your dog.

Dealing with poisoning is tricky because there is no standard treatment. It all depends on the type of poison. For example, in some cases, your dog must be induced to vomit; in others, vomiting can be deadly. For this reason, the wise owner keeps the number of the National Animal Poison Control Center handy at all times and keeps all potential poisons properly stored away from the prying nose of a curious Siberian Husky. (The NAPCC information is in Chapter 13.)

HEATSTROKE

Siberian Huskies are adaptable creatures, but they, like all dogs, will easily succumb to over-heating—which can occur unbelievably quickly. The affected dog will pant rapidly, his mucous membranes will appear bright red, he will be unsteady, and he possibly will vomit. Because your dog's system cannot cool itself, heatstroke is an unconditional life-threatening emergency.

To help cool down the overheated dog, get him quickly to a cool environment (ideally an air-conditioned room, but in a pinch some shade on the trail will suffice). Try to cool his body with cool (not cold) water. The dog's average normal rectal temperature of 101.3° F. can soar as high as 106° F. with heatstroke. **To take your dog's temperature,** clean the rectal thermometer with alcohol, coat it with petroleum jelly, hold up his tail, and gently insert the bulbous end of the thermometer into the anal canal.

Protecting your dog from this life-threatening trauma is simple enough: Schedule exercise sessions during the cooler times of the day; never leave your dog in the car in temperatures that are éven moderately warm (the interior temperature will soar dramatically in minutes, even with the window open); make sure your dog has constant access to plenty of shade and fresh, clean water.

The Older Dog

Thanks to advances in canine care and nutrition, dogs are living longer today than ever before. But as a dog ages, even the healthiest dog, changes occur within his body that herald a new regimen of activity and a new stage in the dog's relationship with his owner.

Living with a puppy is far different from living with a mature five-year-old dog. By the same token, living with that spry five-year-old is quite a bit different from living with that same dog when he reaches his senior years. Dogs age just as humans do, and each life stage offers new joys, new experiences and new health concerns.

Most Siberian Huskies begin to exhibit the telltale signs of aging at about eight to ten years of age. Physically, your dog's muzzle may take on a salt-and-peppery hue (unnoticeable if the dog's muzzle is white); his eyes may begin to reflect the years; and his teeth may begin to yellow, some even requiring extraction (years of dental care is a sound investment in greater tooth health later in life). The greatest sign of aging in the Siberian, however, is in subtle changes in his energy levels.

Aging Well

After many years with a Siberian Husky, most owners learn that this dog tends to retain his youthful exuberance throughout most of his life. Even though the older Siberian may require more hours of sleep each day, when he plays, he still plays as vigorously as he did in his youth. Physical hindrances will ultimately dampen his skills, and it may take longer for your dog to recover following a rousing play session, but his love of the game remains fresh. To retain that freshness, your dog should be allowed to dictate his own activity levels. Trust his instincts.

While it may seem sad to see such an active dog's energy levels wane—to see a robust racing Siberian Husky have to graduate to recreational mushing and finally to just a daily romp in the park—what doesn't change is the bond that that dog shares with his family.

The older dog, especially the older Siberian, may still behave like a five-month-old puppy at times, and that is delightful to see. But when that dog suddenly wants to spend his evenings curled up beside his owner on the couch rather than chasing the other dogs through the house, how can one do anything but revel in this new stage of the relationship?

Keeping that older dog's life as pleasant as possible within this new stage brings new responsibilities to you. The older dog's health becomes more fragile, susceptible to quick deterioration if problems arise. You must then pay even closer attention to subtle changes in physique or behavior that could signal a problem and be attuned to the normal changes caused by aging.

These Siberian Husky puppies are pictures of good health—clear eyes, pink ears, shiny coats—but they need the care and attention of their owners to stay that way and to grow up to be healthy, active dogs.

Routine Care Still Required

The older dog, just like the younger dog, requires routine grooming, regular attention to the teeth and gums and a diet designed for his age. He should still receive his vaccine boosters every year as well as basic routine veterinary care. In fact, because the aging dog is more prone to such conditions as urinary problems, arthritis, old-age cataracts, heart problems and diabetes, visits to your veterinarian twice a year for a geriatric exam, including urinalysis and blood panel, can foster early detection and treatment.

At home, be sensitive to the signals. Your dog may begin to hesitate before going up or down stairs—or refuse to do so completely. The reason? Perhaps a sore back or arthritis in the joints. The older dog may become less tolerant of heat and cold and should be housed accordingly. Even the die-hard, cold-loving Siberian who used to sleep curled in the snow may be pleased to submit to the comforts a warm, dry blanket and a soft bed bring to his aching arthritic joints. Although an outdoor sleeper may suddenly decide to snooze in his formerly unused doghouse, indoors with his family is the ideal niche for an aging Siberian with a newfound appreciation for comfort and warmth.

As your dog ages, he may also begin to lose his sight or hearing—no problem. All he needs to do is call upon his signature Siberian adaptability, and with a bit of consideration from his family, he should get along well. You can even prepare for an eventual loss of sight or hearing by teaching your dog to read hand signals and understand verbal commands. This way, communication can remain effective later on even if your dog loses one of his senses.

Diet Concerns

Diet is another issue critical to the care of the aging dog. It is important to avoid obesity, while making sure your dog receives proper nutrients.

While elderly dogs may thrive best on a special senior or prescription diet, perhaps with supplements prescribed by your veterinarian, some dogs lose their appetites as they get on in years.

If this happens, first have your dog's teeth examined to ensure that mouth pain is not preventing him from eating (if it is, he may have to switch to a softer diet). If all is well with teeth and gums, a dash of garlic or meat broth on the food should help entice this finicky senior citizen to eat. Also helpful is feeding your dog several small meals a day, so as not to overtax the digestive system.

Just as dogs age more quickly than do humans, so can their health begin to deteriorate at a phenomenally quick rate once that process begins. As arthritis sets in, mobility becomes a problem. Anal glands that have remained healthy through normal defecation for so many years may begin to block, requiring routine trips to the veterinarian to clear them or an owner who learns to do it at home. You might find warts or other skin growths on your dog, growths that should be examined by your veterinarian, who can diagnose them as either fatty deposits or tumors.

Age may also take its toll on your dog's bladder or bowel control. If he suddenly diverges from a lifetime perfect record of housetraining, first make sure this is not a sign of a medical problem such as kidney disease or diabetes. If your dog is healthy, commit to taking him out more frequently during the day to give him ample opportunity to eliminate. A new bedding situation may also be in order, one that still retains your dog's comfort, but also makes managing loss of bladder or bowel control easier. Discipline won't work. This is a natural process.

Today this Husky is sitting in a toy wagon; someday he'll be pulling his own sled.

So, no, all about canine aging is not pleasant, but that does not mean that your dog's later years cannot be golden years. Only those who have experienced that special relationship with an aging dog know the magic. So your dog, too, will enjoy that bond, the overriding goal of his care must be to ensure that he remains as comfortable as possible and free from pain and confusion. Given all that is affected by the aging process, this can be an involved, sometimes even heartbreaking, challenge, but one that brings incomparable rewards.

Saying Good-Bye

The time comes in every relationship with a dog when you must say good-bye. After a life of fine care and companionship, we inevitably outlive our dogs. Most who choose to live with dogs know the time must come to make some hard decisions.

While an older dog, even one whose lifestyle has changed dramatically with age, can live for years in comfort and contentment, he will inevitably reach the day when he can no longer sufficiently enjoy his life

The decision for painless, peaceful euthanasia can be one of the most devastating a dog owner is ever asked to make. Once done, it may leave the individual with feelings of loneliness and guilt because dogs, especially dogs as gregarious and people-loving as the Siberian Husky, become important members of the family. But that decision is the only humane option when your dog is suffering badly. Such dear friends deserve compassion and courage from their owners at this critical juncture.

The grieving process is very real when your dog, a longtime family fixture, is no longer around. While outsiders may respond to the loss with such comments as "he was only a dog," you must try to ignore that and allow the grief to play out.

Because many Siberians live in multiple-dog households, the presence of the other dogs can be a comfort. But for the dog that presided over a one-dog domain, the only remedy for the owner he left behind may be in obtaining another dog, not as a replacement, but as a new family member.

Some seek a new canine addition to the family immediately; others must wait until they have completed the grieving process. When and how you obtain a new dog is a very personal decision, one best left not to well-meaning friends who try to surprise their sad friend with a puppy, but to the prospective owner who should choose his or her own companion carefully and in his or her own time.

It is this owner and this dog, after all, who will be sharing the years ahead together in a very special relationship—a relationship the Siberian Husky has enjoyed with humans for thousands of years and will surely continue to enjoy for thousands more.

Your Happy, Healthy Pet

Your Dog's Name _____

Name on Your Dog's Pedigree (if your dog has one) _____

_____

Where Your Dog Came From _____

_____

Your Dog's Birthday _____

Your Dog's Veterinarian

    Name _____

    Address _____

    Phone Number _____

    Emergency Number _____

Your Dog's Health

    Vaccines

    type _____ date given _____

    type _____ date given _____

    type _____ date given _____

    type _____ date given _____

    Heartworm

    date tested _____ type used _____ start date _____

Your Dog's License Number _____

Groomer's Name and Number _____

Dogsitter/Walker's Name and Number _____

Awards Your Dog Has Won

    Award _____ date earned _____

    Award _____ date earned _____

part three

Enjoying your Dog

chapter 8

Basic
Training

by Ian Dunbar, Ph.D., MRCVS

Training is the jewel in the crown—the most important aspect of doggy husbandry. There is no more important variable influencing dog behavior and temperament than the dog's education: A well-trained, well-behaved and good-natured puppydog is always a joy to live with, but an untrained and uncivilized dog can be a perpetual nightmare. Moreover, deny the dog an education and it will not have the opportunity to fulfill its own canine potential; neither will it have the ability to communicate effectively with its human companions.

Luckily, modern psychological training methods are easy, efficient and effective and, above all, considerably dog-friendly and user-friendly. Doggy education is as simple as it is enjoyable. But before you can have a good time play-training with your new dog, you have to learn what to do and how to do it. There is no bigger variable influencing the success of dog training than the *owner's* experience and expertise. *Before you embark on the dog's education, you must first educate yourself.*

Basic Training for Owners

Ideally, basic owner training should begin well *before* you select your dog. Find out all you can about your chosen breed first, then master rudimentary training and handling skills. If you already have your puppy/dog, owner training is a dire emergency—the clock is running! Especially for puppies, the first few weeks at home are the most important and influential days in the dog's life. Indeed, the cause of most adolescent and adult problems may be traced back to the initial days the pup explores his new home. This is the time to establish the *status quo*—to teach the puppy/dog how you would like him to behave and so prevent otherwise quite predictable problems.

In addition to consulting breeders and breed books such as this one (which understandably have a positive breed bias), seek out as many pet owners with your breed you can find. Good points are obvious. What you want to find out are the breed-specific *problems*, so you can nip them in the bud. In particular, you should talk to owners with *adolescent* dogs and make a list of all anticipated problems. Most important, *test drive* at least half a dozen adolescent and adult dogs of your breed yourself. An eight-week-old puppy is deceptively easy to handle, but she will acquire adult size, speed and strength in just four months, so you should learn now what to prepare for.

Puppy and pet dog training classes offer a convenient venue to locate pet owners and observe dogs in action. For a list of suitable trainers in your area, contact the Association of Pet Dog Trainers (see Chapter 13). You may also begin your basic owner training by observing other owners in class. Watch as many classes and test drive as many dogs as possible. Select an upbeat, dog-friendly, people-friendly, fun-and-games, puppydog pet training class to learn the ropes. Also, watch training videos and read training books (see Chapter 12). You must find out what to do and how to do it *before* you have to do it.

Principles of Training

Most people think training comprises teaching the dog to do things such as sit, speak and roll over, but even a four-week-old pup knows how to do these things already. Instead, the first step in training involves teaching the dog human words for each dog behavior and activity and for each aspect of the dog's environment. That way you, the owner, can more easily participate in the dog's domestic education by directing him to perform specific actions appropriately, that is, at the right time, in the right place, and so on. Training opens communication channels, enabling an educated dog to at least understand the owner's requests.

In addition to teaching a dog *what* we want her to do, it is also necessary to teach her *why* she should do what we ask. Indeed, 95 percent of training revolves around motivating the dog *to want to do* what we want. Dogs often understand what their owners want; they just don't see the point of doing it—especially when the owner's repetitively boring and seemingly senseless instructions are totally at odds with much more pressing and exciting doggy distractions. It is not so much the dog who is being stubborn or dominant; rather, it is the owner who has failed to acknowledge the dog's needs and feelings and to approach training from the dog's point of view.

The Meaning of Instructions

The secret to successful training is learning how to use training lures to predict or prompt specific behaviors—to coax the dog to do what you want *when* you want. Any highly valued object (such as a treat or toy) may be used as a lure, which the dog will follow with his eyes and nose. Moving the lure in specific ways entices the dog to move his nose, head and entire body in specific ways. In fact, by learning the art of manipulating various lures, it is possible to teach the dog to assume virtually any body position and perform any action. Once you have control over the expression of the dog's behaviors and can elicit any body position or behavior at will, you can easily teach the dog to perform on request.

Tell your dog what you want him to do, use a lure to entice him to respond correctly, then profusely praise

Teach your dog words for each activity he needs to know, like down.

and maybe reward him once he performs the desired action. For example, verbally request "Fido, sit!" while you move a squeaky toy upwards and backwards over the dog's muzzle (lure-movement and hand signal), smile knowingly as he looks up (to follow the lure) and sits down (as a result of canine anatomical engineering), then praise him to distraction ("Gooood Fido!"). Squeak the toy, offer a training treat and give your dog and yourself a pat on the back.

Being able to elicit desired responses over and over enables the owner to reward the dog over and over. Consequently, the dog begins to think training is fun. For example, the more the dog is rewarded for sitting, the more she enjoys sitting. Eventually the dog comes to realize that, whereas most sitting is appreciated, sitting immediately upon request usually prompts especially enthusiastic praise and a slew of high-level rewards. The dog begins to sit on cue much of the time, showing that she is starting to grasp the meaning of the owner's verbal request and hand signal.

Why Comply?

Most dogs enjoy initial lure/reward training and are only too happy to comply with their owners' wishes. Unfortunately, repetitive drilling without appreciative feedback tends to diminish the dog's enthusiasm until he eventually fails to see the point of complying anymore. Moreover, as the dog approaches adolescence he becomes more easily distracted as he develops other interests. Lengthy sessions with repetitive exercises tend to bore and demotivate both parties. If it's not fun, the owner doesn't do it and neither does the dog.

Integrate training into your dog's life: The greater number of training sessions each day and the *shorter* they are, the more willingly compliant your dog will become. Make sure to have a short (just a few seconds) training interlude before every enjoyable canine activity. For example, ask your dog to sit to greet people, to sit before you throw his Frisbee, and to sit for his supper. Really, sitting is no different from a canine "please." Also, include numerous short training interludes during every enjoyable canine pastime, for example, when playing with the dog or when he is running in the park. In this fashion, doggy distractions may be effectively converted into rewards for training. Just as all games have rules, fun becomes training . . . and training becomes fun.

Eventually, rewards actually become unnecessary to continue motivating your dog. If trained with consideration and kindness, performing the desired behaviors will become self-rewarding and, in a sense, your dog will motivate himself. Just as it is not necessary to reward a human companion during an enjoyable walk in the park, or following a game of tennis, it is hardly necessary to reward our best friend—the dog—for walking by our side or while playing fetch. Human company during enjoyable activities is reward enough for most dogs.

Even though your dog has become self-motivating, it's still good to praise and pet him a lot and offer rewards once in a while, especially for a good job well done. And if for no other reason, praising and rewarding others is good for the human heart.

To train your dog, you need gentle hands, a loving heart and a good attitude.

Punishment

Without a doubt, lure/reward training is by far the best way to teach: Entice your dog to do what you want and then reward him for doing so. Unfortunately, a human shortcoming is to take the good for granted and to moan and groan at the bad. Specifically, the dog's many good behaviors are ignored while the owner focuses on punishing the dog for making mistakes. In extreme cases, instruction is *limited* to punishing mistakes made by a trainee dog, child, employee or husband, even though it has been proven punishment training is notoriously inefficient and ineffective and is decidedly unfriendly and combative. It teaches the dog that training is a drag, almost as quickly as it teaches the dog to dislike his trainer. Why treat our best friends like our worst enemies?

Punishment training is also much more laborious and time consuming. Whereas it takes only a finite amount of time to teach a dog what to chew, for example, it takes much, much longer to punish the dog for each and every mistake. Remember, *there is only one right way!* So why not teach that right way from the outset?!

To make matters worse, punishment training causes severe lapses in the dog's reliability. Since it is obviously impossible to punish the dog each and every time she misbehaves, the dog quickly learns to distinguish between those times when she must comply (so as to avoid impending punishment) and those times when she need not comply, because punishment is impossible. Such times include when the dog is off leash and only six feet away, when the owner is otherwise engaged (talking to a friend, watching television, taking a shower, tending to the baby or chatting on the telephone), or when the dog is left at home alone.

Instances of misbehavior will be numerous when the owner is away, because even when the dog complied in the owner's looming presence, he did so unwillingly. The dog was forced to act against his will, rather than moulding his will to want to please. Hence, when the owner is absent, not only does the dog know he need not comply, he simply does not want to. Again, the trainee is not a stubborn vindictive beast, but rather the trainer has failed to teach.

Punishment training invariably creates unpredictable Jekyll and Hyde behavior.

Trainer's Tools

Many training books extol the virtues of a vast array of training paraphernalia and electronic and metallic gizmos, most of which are designed for canine restraint, correction and punishment, rather than for actual facilitation of doggy education. In reality, most effective training tools are not found in stores; they come from within ourselves. In addition to a willing dog, all you really need is a functional human brain, gentle hands, a loving heart and a good attitude.

In terms of equipment, all dogs do require a quality buckle collar to sport dog tags and to attach the leash (for safety and to comply with local leash laws). Hollow chewtoys (like Kongs or sterilized longbones) and a dog bed or collapsible crate are a must for housetraining. Three additional tools are required:

1. specific lures (training treats and toys) to predict and prompt specific desired behaviors;

2. rewards (praise, affection, training treats and toys) to reinforce for the dog what a lot of fun it all is; and

3. knowledge—how to convert the dog's favorite activities and games (potential distractions to training) into "life-rewards," which may be employed to facilitate training.

The most powerful of these is *knowledge*. Education is the key! Watch training classes, participate in training classes, watch videos, read books, enjoy playtraining with your dog, and then your dog will say "Please," and your dog will say "Thank you!"

Housetraining

If dogs were left to their own devices, certainly they would chew, dig and bark for entertainment and then no doubt highlight a few areas of their living space with sprinkles of urine, in much the same way we decorate by hanging pictures. Consequently, when we ask a dog to live with us, we must teach him *where* he may dig and perform his toilet duties, *what* he may chew and *when* he may bark. After all, when left at home alone for many hours, we cannot expect the dog to amuse himself by completing crosswords or watching the soaps on TV!

Also, it would be decidedly unfair to keep the house rules a secret from the dog, and then get angry and punish the poor critter for inevitably transgressing rules he did not even know existed. Remember, without adequate education and guidance, the dog will be forced to establish his own rules—doggy rules—that most probably will be at odds with the owner's view of domestic living.

Since most problems develop during the first few days the dog is at home, prospective dog owners must be certain they are quite clear about the principles of housetraining *before* they get a dog. Early misbehaviors quickly become established as the status quo—

becoming firmly entrenched as hard-to-break bad habits, which set the precedent for years to come. Make sure to teach your dog good habits right from the start. Good habits are just as hard to break as bad ones!

Ideally, when a new dog comes home, try to arrange for someone to be present for as much as possible during the first few days (for adult dogs) or weeks for puppies. With only a little forethought, it is surprisingly easy to find a puppy sitter, such as a retired person, who would be willing to eat from your refrigerator and watch your television while keeping an eye on the newcomer to encourage the dog to play with chewtoys and to ensure he goes outside on a regular basis.

POTTY TRAINING

To teach the dog where to relieve himself:

1. never let him make a single mistake;
2. let him know where you want him to go; and
3. handsomely reward him for doing so:
   "GOOOOOOOD DOG!!!" liver treat, liver treat, liver treat!

PREVENTING MISTAKES

A single mistake is a training disaster, since it heralds many more in future weeks. And each time the dog soils the house, this further reinforces the dog's unfortunate preference for an indoor, carpeted toilet. *Do not let an unhousetrained dog have full run of the house if you are away from home or cannot pay full attention.* Instead, confine the dog to an area where elimination is appropriate, such as an outdoor run or, better still, a small, comfortable indoor kennel with access to an outdoor run. When confined in this manner, most dogs will naturally housetrain themselves.

If that's not possible, confine the dog to an area, such as a utility room, kitchen, basement or garage, where elimination may not be desired in the long run but as an interim measure it is certainly preferable to doing it all around the house. Use newspaper to cover the floor of the dog's day room. The newspaper may be used to soak up the urine and to wrap up and dispose of the feces. Once your dog develops a preferred spot for eliminating, it is only necessary to cover that part of the floor with newspaper. The smaller papered area may then be moved (only a little each day) towards the door to the outside. Thus the dog will develop the tendency to go to the door when he needs to relieve himself.

Never confine an unhousetrained dog to a crate for long periods. Doing so would force the dog to soil the crate and ruin its usefulness as an aid for housetraining (see the following discussion).

The first few weeks at home are the most important and influential in your dog's life.

TEACHING WHERE

In order to teach your dog where you would like her to do her business, you have to be there to direct the proceedings—an obvious, yet often neglected, fact of life. In order to be there to teach the dog *where* to go, you need to know *when* she needs to go. Indeed, the success of housetraining depends on the owner's ability to predict these times. Certainly, a regular feeding schedule will facilitate prediction somewhat, but there is nothing like "loading the deck" and influencing the timing of the outcome yourself!

Whenever you are at home, make sure the dog is under constant supervision and/or confined to a small area. If already well trained, simply instruct the dog to lie down in his bed or basket. Alternatively, confine the dog to a crate (doggy den) or tie-down (a short, 18-inch lead that can be clipped to an eye hook in the baseboard). Short-term close confinement strongly inhibits urination and defecation, since the dog does not want to soil his sleeping area. Thus, when you release the puppydog each hour, he will definitely need to urinate immediately and defecate every third or fourth hour. Keep the dog confined to his doggy den and take him to his intended toilet area each hour, every hour, and on the hour.

When taking your dog outside, instruct him to sit quietly before opening the door—he will soon learn to sit by the door when he needs to go out!

TEACHING WHY

Being able to predict when the dog needs to go enables the owner to be on the spot to praise and reward the dog. Each hour, hurry the dog to the intended toilet area in the yard, issue the appropriate instruction ("Go pee!" or "Go poop!"), then give the dog three to four minutes to produce. Praise and offer a couple of training treats when successful. The treats are important because many people fail to praise their dogs with feeling . . . and housetraining is hardly the time for understatement. So either loosen up and enthusiastically praise that dog: "Wuzzzer-wuzzer-wuzzer, hoooser good wuffer den? Hoooo went pee for Daddy?" Or say "Good dog!" as best you can and offer the treats for effect.

Following elimination is an ideal time for a spot of playtraining in the yard or house. Also, an empty dog may be allowed greater freedom around the house for the next half hour or so, just as long as you keep an eye out to make sure he does not get into other kinds of mischief. If you are preoccupied and cannot pay full attention, confine the dog to his doggy den once more to enjoy a peaceful snooze or to play with his many chewtoys.

If your dog does not eliminate within the allotted time outside—no biggie! Back to his doggy den, and then try again after another hour.

As I own large dogs, I always feel more relaxed walking an empty dog, knowing that I will not need to finish our stroll weighted down with bags of feces! Beware of falling into the trap of walking the dog to get it to eliminate. The good ol' dog walk is such an enormous highlight in the dog's life that it represents the single biggest potential reward in domestic dogdom. However, when in a hurry, or during inclement weather, many owners abruptly terminate the walk the moment the dog has done its business. This, in effect, severely punishes the dog for doing the right thing, in the right place at the right time. Consequently, many dogs become strongly inhibited from eliminating outdoors because they know it will signal an abrupt end to an otherwise thoroughly enjoyable walk.

Instead, instruct the dog to relieve himself in the yard prior to going for a walk. If you follow the above instructions, most dogs soon learn to eliminate on cue. As soon as the dog eliminates, praise (and offer a treat or two)—"Good dog! Let's go walkies!" Use the walk as a reward for eliminating in the yard. If the dog does not go, put him back in his doggy den and think about a walk later on. You will find with a "No feces–no walk" policy, your dog will become one of the fastest defecators in the business.

If you do not have a back yard, instruct the dog to eliminate right outside your front door prior to the walk. Not only will this facilitate clean up and disposal of the feces in your own trash can but, also, the walk may again be used as a colossal reward.

Chewing and Barking

Short-term close confinement also teaches the dog that occasional quiet moments are a reality of domestic living. Your puppydog is extremely impressionable during his first few weeks at home. Regular confinement at this time soon exerts a calming influ-ence over the dog's personality. Remember, once the dog is housetrained and calmer, there will be a whole lifetime ahead for the dog to enjoy full run of the house and garden. On the other hand, by letting the newcomer have unrestricted access to the entire house-hold and allowing him to run willy-nilly, he will most certainly develop a bunch of behavior problems in short order, no doubt necessitating confinement later in life. It would not be fair to remedially restrain and confine a dog you have trained, through neglect, to run free.

When confining the dog, make sure he always has an impressive array of suitable chewtoys. Kongs and steril-ized longbones (both readily available from pet stores) make the best chewtoys, since they are hollow and may be stuffed with treats to heighten the dog's interest. For example, by stuffing the little hole at the top of a Kong with a small piece of freeze-dried liver, the dog will not want to leave it alone.

Remember, treats do not have to be junk food and they certainly should not represent extra calories. Rather, treats should be part of each dog's regular daily diet:

Make sure your puppy has suitable chewtoys.

Some food may be served in the dog's bowl for breakfast and dinner, some food may be used as train-ing treats, and some food may be used for stuffing chewtoys. I regularly stuff my dogs' many Kongs with different shaped biscuits and kibble. The kibble seems to fall out fairly easily, as do the oval-shaped biscuits, thus rewarding the dog instanta-neously for checking out the chewtoys. The bone-shaped biscuits fall out after a while, rewarding the dog for worrying at the chewtoy. But the triangular biscuits never come out. They remain inside the Kong as lures, maintaining the dog's fascination with its chewtoy. To further focus the dog's interest, I always make sure to flavor the triangular biscuits by rubbing them with a little cheese or freeze-dried liver.

If stuffed chewtoys are reserved especially for times the dog is confined, the puppy-dog will soon learn to enjoy quiet moments in her doggy den and she will quickly develop a chewtoy habit—a good habit! This is a simple *passive training* process; all the owner has to do is set up the situation and the dog all but trains herself—easy and effective. Even when the dog is given run of the house, her first inclination will be to indulge her rewarding chewtoy habit rather than destroying less-attractive household articles, such as curtains, carpets, chairs and compact disks. Similarly, a chewtoy chewer will be less inclined to scratch and chew herself excessively. Also, if the dog busies herself as a recreational chewer, she will be less inclined to develop into a recreational barker or digger when left at home alone.

Stuff a number of chewtoys whenever the dog is left confined and remove the extra-special-tasting treats when you return. Your dog will now amuse himself with his chewtoys before falling asleep and then resume playing with his chewtoys when he expects you to return. Since most owner-absent misbehavior happens right after you leave and right before your expected return, your puppydog will now be conveniently preoccupied with his chewtoys at these times.

Come and Sit

Most puppies will happily approach virtually anyone, whether called or not; that is, until they collide with

To teach come, call your dog, open your arms as a welcoming signal, wave a toy or a treat and praise for every step in your direction.

adolescence and develop other more important doggy interests, such as sniffing a multiplicity of exquisite odors on the grass. Your mission, Mr. and/or Ms. Owner, is to teach and reward the pup for coming reliably, willingly and happily when called—and you have just three months to get it done. Unless adequately reinforced, your puppy's tendency to approach people will self-destruct by adolescence.

Call your dog ("Fido, come!"), open your arms (and maybe squat down) as a welcoming signal, waggle a treat or toy as a lure, and reward the puppydog when he comes running. Do not wait to praise the dog until he reaches you—he may come 95 percent of the way and then run off after some distraction. Instead, praise the dog's *first* step towards you and continue praising enthusiastically for *every* step he takes in your direction.

When the rapidly approaching puppy dog is three lengths away from impact, instruct him to sit ("Fido, sit!") and hold the lure in front of you in an outstretched hand to prevent him from hitting you mid-chest and knocking you flat on your back! As Fido decelerates to nose the lure, move the treat upwards and backwards just over his muzzle with an upwards motion of your extended arm (palm-upwards). As the dog looks up to follow the lure, he will sit down (if he jumps up, you are holding the lure too high). Praise the dog for sitting. Move backwards and call him again. Repeat this many times over, always praising when Fido comes and sits; on occasion, reward him.

For the first couple of trials, use a training treat both as a lure to entice the dog to come and sit and as a reward for doing so. Thereafter, try to use different items as lures and rewards. For example, lure the dog with a Kong or Frisbee but reward her with a food treat. Or lure the dog with a food treat but pat her and throw a tennis ball as a reward. After just a few repetitions, dispense with the lures and rewards; the dog will begin to respond willingly to your verbal requests and hand signals just for the prospect of praise from your heart and affection from your hands.

Instruct every family member, friend and visitor how to get the dog to come and sit. Invite people over for a series of pooch parties; do not keep the pup a secret— let other people enjoy this puppy, and let the pup enjoy other people. Puppydog parties are not only fun, they easily attract a lot of people to help *you* train *your* dog. Unless you teach your dog *how* to meet people, that is, to sit for greetings, no doubt the dog will resort to jumping up. Then you and the visitors will get annoyed, and the dog will be punished. This is not fair. *Send out those invitations for puppy parties and teach your dog to be mannerly and socially acceptable.*

Even though your dog quickly masters obedient recalls in the house, his reliability may falter when playing in the back yard or local park. Ironically, it is *the owner* who has unintentionally trained the dog *not* to respond in these instances. By allowing the dog to play and run around and otherwise have a good time, but then to call the dog to put him on leash to take him home, the dog quickly learns playing is fun but training is a drag. Thus, playing in the park becomes a severe distraction, which works against training. Bad news!

Instead, whether playing with the dog off leash or on leash, request him to come at frequent intervals— say, every minute or so. On most occasions, praise and pet the dog for a few seconds while he is sitting, then tell him to go play again. For especially fast recalls, offer a couple of training treats and take the time to praise and pet the dog enthusiastically before releasing him. The dog will learn that coming when called is not necessarily the end of the play session, and neither is it the end of the world; rather, it signals an enjoyable, quality time-out with the owner before resuming play once more. In fact, playing in the park now becomes a very effective life-reward, which works to facilitate training by reinforcing each obedient and timely recall. Good news!

Sit, Down, Stand and Rollover

Teaching the dog a variety of body positions is easy for owner and dog, impressive for spectators and extremely useful for all. Using lure-reward techniques, it is possible to train several positions at once to verbal commands or hand signals (which impress the socks off onlookers).

Sit and *down*—the two control commands—prevent or resolve nearly a hundred behavior problems. For example, if the dog happily and obediently sits or lies down when requested, he cannot jump on visitors, dash out the front door, run around and chase its tail, pester other dogs, harass cats or annoy family, friends or strangers. Additionally, "sit" or "down" are better emergency commands for off-leash control.

It is easier to teach and maintain a reliable sit than maintain a reliable recall. *Sit* is the purest and simplest of commands—either the dog is sitting or he is not. If there is any change of circumstances or potential danger in the park, for example, simply instruct the dog to sit. If he sits, you have a number of options: allow the dog to resume playing when he is safe; walk up and put the dog on leash, or call the dog. The dog will be much more likely to come when called if he has already acknowledged his compliance by sitting. If the dog does not sit in the park—train him to!

Stand and *rollover-stay* are the two positions for examining the dog. Your veterinarian will love you to distraction if you take a little time to teach the dog to stand still and roll over and play possum. Also, your vet bills will be smaller. The rollover-stay is an especially useful command and is really just a variation of the down-stay: whereas the dog lies prone in the traditional down, she lies supine in the rollover-stay.

As with teaching come and sit, the training techniques to teach the dog to assume all other body positions on cue are user-friendly and dog-friendly. Simply give the appropriate request, lure the dog into the desired body position using a training treat or toy and then *praise* (and maybe reward) the dog as soon as he complies. Try not to touch the dog to get him to respond. If you teach the dog by guiding him into position, the dog will quickly learn that rump-pressure means sit, for example, but as yet you still have no control over your dog if he is just six feet away. It will still be necessary to teach the dog to sit on request. So do not make training a time-consuming two-step process; instead, teach the dog to sit to a verbal request or hand signal from the outset. Once the dog sits willingly when requested, by all means use your hands to pet the dog when he does so.

To teach *down* when the dog is already sitting, say "Fido, down!," hold the lure in one hand (palm down) and lower that hand to the floor between the dog's forepaws. As the dog lowers his head to follow the lure, slowly move the lure away from the dog just a fraction (in front of his paws). The dog will lie down as he stretches his nose forward to follow the lure. Praise the dog when he does so. If the dog stands up, you pulled the lure away too far and too quickly.

When teaching the dog to lie down from the standing position, say "down" and lower the lure to the floor as before. Once the dog has lowered his forequarters and assumed a play bow, gently and slowly move the lure *towards* the dog between his forelegs. Praise the dog as soon as his rear end plops down.

After just a couple of trials it will be possible to alternate sits and downs and have the dog energetically perform doggy push-ups. Praise the dog a lot, and after half a dozen or so push-ups reward the dog with a training treat or toy. You will notice the more energetically you move your arm—upwards (palm up) to get the dog to sit, and downwards (palm down) to get the dog to lie down—the more energetically the dog responds to your requests. Now try training the dog in silence and you will notice he has also learned to respond to hand signals. Yeah! Not too shabby for the first session.

To teach *stand* from the sitting position, say "Fido, stand," slowly move the lure half a dog-length away from the dog's nose, keeping it at nose level, and praise the dog as he stands to follow the lure. As soon

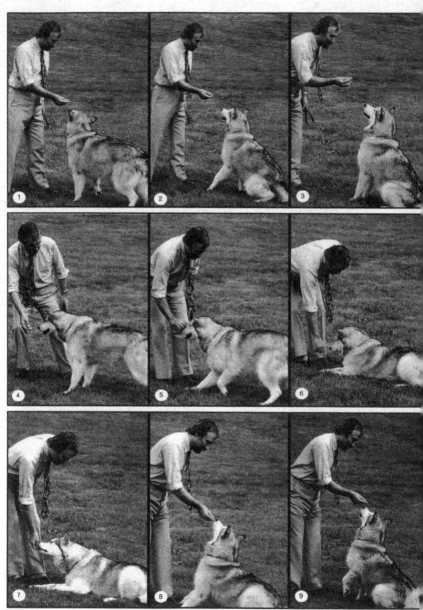

Using a food lure to teach sit, down and stand. 1) "Phoenix, Sit." 2) Hand palm upwards, move lure up and back over dog's muzzle. 3) "Good sit, Phoenix!" 4) "Phoenix, down." 5) Hand palm downwards, move lure down to lie between dog's forepaws. 6) "Phoenix, off. Good down, Phoenix!" 7) "Phoenix, sit!" 8) Palm upwards, move lure up and back, keeping it close to dog's muzzle. 9) "Good sit, Phoenix!

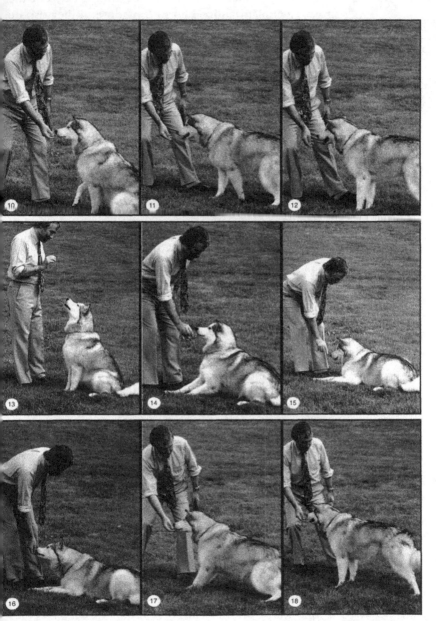

10) "Phoenix, stand!" 11) Move lure away from dog at nose height, then lower it a tad. 12) "Phoenix, off! Good stand, Phoenix!" 13) "Phoenix, down!" 14) Hand palm downwards, move lure down to lie between dog's forepaws. 15) "Phoenix, off! Good down-stay, Phoenix!" 16) "Phoenix, stand!" 17) Move lure away from dog's muzzle up to nose height. 18) "Phoenix,off! Good stand-stay, Phoenix. Now we'll make the vet and groomer happy!"

as the dog stands, lower the lure to just beneath the dog's chin to entice him to look down; otherwise he will stand and then sit immediately. To prompt the dog to stand from the down position, move the lure half a dog-length upwards and away from the dog, holding the lure at standing nose height from the floor.

Teaching *rollover* is best started from the down position, with the dog lying on one side, or at least with both hind legs stretched out on the same side. Say "Fido, bang!" and move the lure backwards and alongside the dog's muzzle to its elbow (on the side of its outstretched hind legs). Once the dog looks to the side and backwards, very slowly move the lure upwards to the dog's shoulder and backbone. Tickling the dog in the goolies (groin area) often invokes a reflex-raising of the hind leg as an appeasement gesture, which facilitates the tendency to roll over. If you move the lure too quickly and the dog jumps into the standing position, have patience and start again. As soon as the dog rolls onto its back, keep the lure stationary and mesmerize the dog with a relaxing tummy rub.

To teach *rollover-stay* when the dog is standing or moving, say "Fido, bang!" and give the appropriate hand signal (with index finger pointed and thumb cocked in true Sam Spade fashion), then in one fluid movement lure him to first lie down and then rollover-stay as above.

Teaching the dog to *stay* in each of the above four positions becomes a piece of cake after first teaching the dog not to worry at the toy or treat training lure. This is best accomplished by hand feeding dinner kibble. Hold a piece of kibble firmly in your hand and softly instruct "Off!" Ignore any licking and slobbering *for however long the dog worries at the treat*, but say "Take it!" and offer the kibble *the instant* the dog breaks contact with his muzzle. Repeat this a few times, and then up the ante and insist the dog remove his muzzle for one whole second before offering the kibble. Then progressively refine your criteria and have the dog not touch your hand (or treat) for longer and longer periods on each trial, such as for two seconds, four seconds, then six, ten, fifteen, twenty, thirty seconds and so on. The dog soon learns: (1) worrying at the treat never gets results, whereas (2) noncontact is often rewarded after a variable time lapse.

Teaching *"Off!"* has many useful applications in its own right. Additionally, instructing the dog not to touch a training lure often produces spontaneous and magical stays. Request the dog to stand-stay, for example, and not to touch the lure. At first set your sights on a short two-second stay before rewarding the dog. (Remember, every long journey begins with a single step.) However, on subsequent trials, gradually and progressively increase the length of stay required to receive a reward. In no time at all your dog will stand calmly for a minute or so.

Relevancy Training

Once you have taught the dog what you expect her to do when requested to come, sit, lie down, stand, rollover and stay, the time is right to teach the dog *why* she should comply with your wishes. The secret is to have many (*many*) extremely short training interludes (two to five seconds each) at numerous (*numerous*) times during the course of the dog's day. Especially work with the dog immediately *before* the dog's good times and *during* the dog's good times. For example, ask your dog to sit and/or lie down each time before opening doors, serving meals, offering treats and tummy rubs; ask the dog to perform a few controlled doggy push-ups before letting her off-leash or throwing a tennis ball; and perhaps request the dog to sit-down-sit-stand-down-stand-rollover before inviting her to cuddle on the couch.

Similarly, request the dog to sit many times during play or on walks, and in no time at all the dog will be only too pleased to follow your instructions because he has learned that a compliant response heralds all sorts of goodies. Basically all you are trying to teach the dog is how to say please: "Please throw the tennis ball. Please may I snuggle on the couch."

Remember, whereas it is important to keep training interludes short, it is equally important to have many short sessions each and every day. The shortest (and most useful) session comprises asking the dog to sit and then go play during a play session. When trained this way, your dog will soon associate training with good times. In fact, the dog may be unable to distinguish between training and good times and, indeed, there should be no distinction. The warped concept that training involves forcing the dog to comply and/or dominating his will is totally at odds with the picture of a truly well-trained dog. In reality, enjoying a game of training with a dog is no different from enjoying a game of backgammon or tennis with a friend; and walking with a dog should be no different from strolling with buddies on the golf course.

Walk by Your Side

Many people attempt to teach a dog to heel by putting him on a leash and physically correcting the dog when he makes mistakes. There are a number of things seriously wrong with this approach, the first being that most people do not want precision heeling; rather, they simply want the dog to follow or walk by their side. Second, when physically restrained during "training," even though the dog may grudgingly mope by your side when "handcuffed" on leash, let's see what happens when he is off leash. History! The dog is in the next county because he never enjoyed walking with you on leash and you have no control over him off leash. So let's just teach the dog off leash from the outset to *want* to walk with us. Third, if the dog has not been trained to heel, it is a trifle hasty to think about punishing the poor dog for making mistakes and breaking heeling rules he didn't even know existed. This is simply not fair! Surely, if the dog had been adequately taught how to heel, he would seldom make mistakes and hence there would be no need to correct the dog. Remember, each mistake and each correction (punishment) advertise the trainer's inadequacy, not the dog's. The dog is not stubborn, he is not stupid and he is not bad. Even if he were, he would still require training, so let's train him properly.

Let's teach the dog to *enjoy* following us and to *want* to walk by our side offleash. Then it will be easier to teach high-precision off-leash heeling patterns if desired. After attaching the leash for safety on outdoor walks, but before going anywhere, it is necessary to teach the dog specifically not to pull. Now it will be much easier to teach on-leash walking and heeling because the dog already wants to walk with you, he is familiar with the desired walking and heeling positions and he knows not to pull.

FOLLOWING

Start by training your dog to follow you. Many puppies will follow if you simply walk away from them and maybe click your fingers or chuckle. Adult dogs may require additional enticement to stimulate them to follow, such as a training lure or, at the very least, a lively trainer. To teach the dog to follow: (1) keep walking and (2) walk away from the dog. If the dog attempts to lead or lag, change pace; slow down if the dog forges too far ahead, but speed up if he lags too far behind. Say "Steady!" or "Easy!" each time before you slow down and "Quickly!" or "Hustle!" each time before you speed up, and the dog will learn to change pace on cue. If the dog lags or leads too far, or if he wanders right or left, simply walk quickly in the opposite direction and maybe even run away from the dog and hide.

Practicing is a lot of fun; you can set up a course in your home, yard or park to do this. Indoors, entice the dog to follow upstairs, into a bedroom, into the bathroom, downstairs, around the living room couch, zigzagging between dining room chairs and into the kitchen for dinner. Outdoors, get the dog to follow around park benches, trees, shrubs and along walkways and lines in the grass. (For safety outdoors, it is advisable to attach a long line on the dog, but never exert corrective tension on the line.)

Remember, following has a lot to do with attitude—
your attitude! Most probably your dog will *not* want to
follow Mr. Grumpy Troll with the personality of wilted
lettuce. Lighten up—walk with a jaunty step, whistle a
happy tune, sing, skip and tell jokes to your dog and he
will be right there by your side.

BY YOUR SIDE

It is smart to train the dog to walk close on one side or
the other—either side will do, your choice. When walking, jogging or cycling, it is generally bad news to have
the dog suddenly cut in front of you. In fact, I train my
dogs to walk "By my side" and "Other side"—both very
useful instructions. It is possible to position the dog
fairly accurately by looking to the appropriate side and
clicking your fingers or slapping your thigh on that
side. A precise positioning may be attained by holding
a training lure, such as a chewtoy, tennis ball, or food
treat. Stop and stand still several times throughout the
walk, just as you would when window shopping or
meeting a friend. Use the lure to make sure the dog
slows down and stays close whenever you stop.

When teaching the dog to heel, we generally want
her to sit in heel position when we stop. Teach heel

Using a toy to teach sit-heel-sit sequences: 1) "Phoenix, heel!" Standing still, move lure up and ba
over dog's muzzle.... 2) To position dog sitting in heel position on your left side. 3) "Phoenix, heel.
wagging lure in left hand. Change lure to right hand in preparation for sit signal.

position at the standstill and the dog will learn that the default heel position is sitting by your side (left or right—your choice, unless you wish to compete in obedience trials, in which case the dog must heel on the left).

Several times a day, stand up and call your dog to come and sit in heel position—"Fido, heel!" For example, instruct the dog to come to heel each time there are commercials on TV, or each time you turn a page of a novel, and the dog will get it in a single evening.

Practice straight-line heeling and turns separately. With the dog sitting at heel, teach him to turn in place. After each quarter-turn, half turn or full turn in place, lure the dog to sit at heel. Now it's time for short straight-line heeling sequences, no more than a few steps at a time. Always think of heeling in terms of Sit-Heel-Sit sequences—start and end with the dog in position and do your best to keep him there when moving. Progressively increase the number of steps in each sequence. When the dog remains close for 20 yards of straight-line heeling, it is time to add a few turns and then sign up for a happy-heeling obedience class to get some advice from the experts.

4) Use hand signal only to lure dog to sit as you stop. Eventually, dog will sit automatically at heel whenever you stop. 5) "Good dog!"

NO PULLING ON LEASH

You can start teaching your dog not to pull on leash anywhere—in front of the television or outdoors—but regardless of location, you must not take a single step with tension in the leash. For a reason known only to dogs, even just a couple of paces of pulling on leash is intrinsically motivating and diabolically rewarding. Instead, attach the leash to the dog's collar, grasp the other end firmly with both hands held close to your chest, and stand still—do not budge an inch. Have somebody watch you with a stopwatch to time your progress, or else you will never believe this will work and so you will not even try the exercise, and your shoulder and the dog's neck will be traumatized for years to come.

Stand still and wait for the dog to stop pulling, and to sit and/or lie down. All dogs stop pulling and sit eventually. Most take only a couple of minutes; the all-time record is 22 $\frac{1}{5}$ minutes. Time how long it takes. Gently praise the dog when he stops pulling, and as soon as he sits, enthusiastically praise the dog and take just one step forwards, then immediately stand still. This single step usually demonstrates the ballistic reinforcing nature of pulling on leash; most dogs explode to the end of the leash, so be prepared for the strain. Stand firm and wait for the dog to sit again. Repeat this half a dozen times and you will probably notice a progressive reduction in the force of the dog's one-step explosions and a radical reduction in the time it takes for the dog to sit each time.

As the dog learns "Sit we go" and "Pull we stop," she will begin to walk forward calmly with each single step and automatically sit when you stop. Now try two steps before you stop. Wooooooo! Scary! When the dog has mastered two steps at a time, try for three. After each success, progressively increase the number of steps in the sequence: try four steps and then six, eight, ten and twenty steps before stopping. Congratulations! You are now walking the dog on leash.

Whenever walking with the dog (off leash or on leash), make sure you stop periodically to practice a few position commands and stays before instructing the dog to "Walk on!" (Remember, you want the dog to be compliant everywhere, not just in the kitchen when his dinner is at hand.) For example, stopping every 25 yards to briefly train the dog amounts to over 200 training interludes within a single three-mile stroll. And each training session is in a different location. You will not believe the improvement within just the first mile of the first walk.

To put it another way, integrating training into a walk offers 200 separate opportunities to use the continuance of the walk as a reward to reinforce the dog's education. Moreover, some training interludes may comprise continuing education for the dog's walking skills: Alternate short periods of the dog walking calmly by your side with periods when the dog is allowed to sniff and investigate the environment. Now sniffing odors on the grass and meeting other dogs become rewards which reinforce the dog's calm and mannerly demeanor. Good Lord! Whatever next? Many enjoyable walks together of course. Happy trails!

THE IMPORTANCE OF TRICKS

Nothing will improve a dog's quality of life better than having a few tricks under its belt. Teaching any trick expands the dog's vocabulary, which facilitates communication and improves the owner's control. Also, specific tricks help prevent and resolve specific behavior problems. For example, by teaching the dog to fetch his toys, the dog learns carrying a toy makes the owner happy and, therefore, will be more likely to chew his toy than other inappropriate items.

More important, teaching tricks prompts owners to lighten up and train with a sunny disposition. Really, tricks should be no different from any other behaviors we put on cue. But they are. When teaching tricks, owners have a much sweeter attitude, which in turn motivates the dog and improves her willingness to comply. The dog feels tricks are a blast, but formal commands are a drag. In fact, tricks are so enjoyable, they may be used as rewards in training by asking the dog to come, sit and down-stay and then rollover for a tummy rub. Go on, try it: Crack a smile and even giggle when the dog promptly and willingly lies down and stays.

Most important, performing tricks prompts onlookers to smile and gig-gle. Many people are scared of dogs, especially large ones. And noth-ing can be more off-putting for a dog than to be constantly confronted by strangers who don't like him because of his size or the way he looks. Uneasy people put the dog on edge, causing him to back off and bark, only frightening people all the more. And so a vicious circle develops, with the people's fear fueling the dog's fear *and vice versa*. Instead, tie a pink ribbon to your dog's collar and practice all sorts of tricks on walks and in the park, and you will be pleasantly amazed how it changes people's attitudes toward your friendly dog. The dog's reper-toire of tricks is limited only by the trainer's imagination. Below I have described three of my favorites:

SPEAK AND SHUSH

The training sequence involved in teaching a dog to bark on request is no different from that used when training any behavior on cue: request—lure—response—reward. As always, the secret of success lies in finding an effective lure. If the dog always barks at the doorbell, for example, say "Rover, speak!", have an accomplice ring the doorbell, then reward the dog for barking. After a few woofs, ask Rover to "Shush!", waggle a food treat under his nose (to entice him to sniff and thus to shush), praise him when quiet and eventually offer the treat as a reward. Alternate "Speak" and "Shush," progressively increasing the length of shush-time between each barking bout.

PLAYBOW

With the dog standing, say "Bow!" and lower the food lure (palm upwards) to rest between the dog's forepaws. Praise as the dog lowers

her forequarters and sternum to the ground (as when teaching the down), but then lure the dog to stand and offer the treat. On successive trials, gradually increase the length of time the dog is required to remain in the playbow posture in order to gain a food reward. If the dog's rear end collapses into a down, say nothing and offer no reward; simply start over.

BE A BEAR

With the dog sitting backed into a corner to prevent him from toppling over backwards, say "Be a Bear!" With bent paw and palm down, raise a lure upwards and backwards along the top of the dog's muzzle. Praise the dog when he sits up on his haunches and offer the treat as a reward. To prevent the dog from standing on his hind legs, keep the lure closer to the dog's muzzle. On each trial, progressively increase the length of time the dog is required to sit up to receive a food reward. Since lure/reward training is so easy, teach the dog to stand and walk on his hind legs as well!

Teaching "Be a Bear"

chapter 9

Getting
Active
with your Dog

by Bardi McLennan

Once you and your dog have graduated from basic obedience training and are beginning to work together as a team, you can take part in the growing world of dog activities. There are so many fun things to do with your dog! Just remember, people and dogs don't always learn at the same pace, so don't be upset if you (or your dog) need more than two basic training courses before your team becomes operational. Even smart dogs don't go straight to college from kindergarten!

Just as there are events geared to certain types of dogs, so there are ones that are more appealing to certain types of people. In some activities, you give the commands and your dog does the work (upland game hunting is one example), while in others, such as agility, you'll both get a workout. You may want to aim for prestigious titles to add to your dog's name, or you may want nothing more than the sheer enjoyment of being around other people and their dogs. Passive or active, participation has its own rewards.

Consider your dog's physical capabilities when looking into any of the canine activities. It's easy to see that a Basset Hound is not built for the racetrack, nor would a Chihuahua be the breed of choice for pulling a sled. A loyal dog will attempt almost anything you ask him to do, so it is up to you to know your

dog's limitations. A dog must be physically sound in order to compete at any level in athletic activities, and being mentally sound is a definite plus. Advanced age, however, may not be a deterrent. Many dogs still hunt and herd at ten or twelve years of age. It's entirely possible for dogs to be "fit at 50." Take your dog for a checkup, explain to your vet the type of activity you have in mind and be guided by his or her findings.

All dogs seem to love playing flyball.

You needn't be restricted to breed-specific sports if it's only fun you're after. Certain AKC activities are limited to designated breeds; however, as each new trial, test or sport has grown in popularity, so has the variety of breeds encouraged to participate at a fun level.

But don't shortchange your fun, or that of your dog, by thinking only of the basic function of her breed. Once a dog has learned how to learn, she can be taught to do just about anything as long as the size of the dog is right for the job and you both think it is fun and rewarding. In other words, you are a team.

To get involved in any of the activities detailed in this chapter, look for the names and addresses of the organizations that sponsor them in Chapter 13. You can also ask your breeder or a local dog trainer for contacts.

You can compete in obedience trials with a well trained dog.

Official American Kennel Club Activities

The following tests and trials are some of the events sanctioned by the AKC and sponsored by various dog clubs. Your dog's expertise will be rewarded with impressive titles. You can participate just for fun, or be competitive and go for those awards.

OBEDIENCE

Training classes begin with pups as young as three months of age in kindergarten puppy training, then advance to pre-novice (all exercises on lead) and go on to novice, which is where you'll start off-lead work. In obedience classes dogs learn to sit, stay, heel and come through a variety of exercises. Once you've got the basics down, you can enter obedience trials and work toward earning your dog's first degree, a C.D. (Companion Dog).

The next level is called "Open," in which jumps and retrieves perk up the dog's interest. Passing grades in competition at this level earn a C.D.X. (Companion Dog Excellent). Beyond that lies the goal of the most ambitious—Utility (U.D. and even U.D.X. or OTCh, an Obedience Champion).

AGILITY

All dogs can participate in the latest canine sport to have gained worldwide popularity for its fun and excitement, agility. It began in England as a canine version of horse show-jumping, but because dogs are more agile and able to perform on verbal commands, extra feats were added such as climbing, balancing and racing through tunnels or in and out of weave poles. Many of the obstacles (regulation or homemade) can be set up in your own backyard. If the agility bug bites, you could end up in international competition!

For starters, your dog should be obedience trained, even though, in the beginning, the lessons may all be taught on lead. Once the dog understands the commands (and you do, too), it's as easy as guiding the dog over a prescribed course, one obstacle at a time. In competition, the race is against the clock, so wear your running shoes! The dog starts with 200 points and the judge deducts for infractions and misadventures along the way.

All dogs seem to love agility and respond to it as if they were being turned loose in a playground paradise. Your dog's enthusiasm will be contagious; agility turns into great fun for dog and owner.

FIELD TRIALS AND HUNTING TESTS

There are field trials and hunting tests for the sporting breeds—retrievers, spaniels and pointing breeds, and for some hounds—Bassets, Beagles and Dachshunds. Field trials are competitive events that test a dog's ability to perform the functions for which she was bred. Hunting tests, which are open to retrievers,

TITLES AWARDED BY THE AKC

Conformation: Ch. (Champion)

Obedience: CD (Companion Dog); CDX (Companion Dog Excellent); UD (Utility Dog); UDX (Utility Dog Excellent); OTCh. (Obedience Trial Champion)

Field: JH (Junior Hunter); SH (Senior Hunter); MH (Master Hunter); AFCh. (Amateur Field Champion); FCh. (Field Champion)

Lure Coursing: JC (Junior Courser); SC (Senior Courser)

Herding: HT (Herding Tested); PT (Pre-Trial Tested); HS (Herding Started); HI (Herding Intermediate); HX (Herding Excellent); HCh. (Herding Champion)

Tracking: TD (Tracking Dog); TDX (Tracking Dog Excellent)

Agility: NAD (Novice Agility); OAD (Open Agility); ADX (Agility Excellent); MAX (Master Agility)

Earthdog Tests: JE (Junior Earthdog); SE (Senior Earthdog); ME (Master Earthdog)

Canine Good Citizen: CGC

Combination: DC (Dual Champion—Ch. and Fch.); TC (Triple Champion—Ch., Fch., and OTCh.)

spaniels and pointing breeds only, are noncompetitive and are a means of judging the dog's ability as well as that of the handler.

Hunting is a very large and complex part of canine sports, and if you own one of the breeds that hunts, the events are a great treat for your dog and you. He gets to do what he was bred for, and you get to work with him and watch him do it. You'll be proud of and amazed at what your dog can do.

Fortunately, the AKC publishes a series of booklets on these events, which outline the rules and regulations and include a glossary of the sometimes complicated terms. The AKC also publishes newsletters for field trialers and hunting test enthusiasts. The United Kennel Club (UKC) also has informative materials for the hunter and his dog.

Retrievers and other sporting breeds get to do what they're bred to in hunting tests.

HERDING TESTS AND TRIALS

Herding, like hunting, dates back to the first known uses man made of dogs. The interest in herding today is widespread, and if you own a herding breed, you can join in the activity. Herding dogs are tested for their natural skills to keep a flock of ducks, sheep or cattle together. If your dog shows potential, you can start at the testing level, where your dog can

earn a title for showing an inherent herding ability. With training you can advance to the trial level, where your dog should be capable of controlling even difficult livestock in diverse situations.

LURE COURSING

The AKC Tests and Trials for Lure Coursing are open to traditional sighthounds—Greyhounds, Whippets,

Borzoi, Salukis, Afghan Hounds, Ibizan Hounds and Scottish Deerhounds—as well as to Basenjis and Rhodesian Ridgebacks. Hounds are judged on overall ability, follow, speed, agility and endurance. This is possibly the most exciting of the trials for spectators, because the speed and agility of the dogs is awesome to watch as they chase the lure (or "course") in heats of two or three dogs at a time.

TRACKING

Tracking is another activity in which almost any dog can compete because every dog that sniffs the ground when taken outdoors is, in fact, tracking. The hard part comes when the rules as to what, when and where the dog tracks are determined by a person, not the dog! Tracking tests cover a large area of fields, woods and roads. The tracks are laid hours before the dogs go to work on them, and include "tricks" like cross-tracks and sharp turns. If you're interested in search-and-rescue work, this is the place to start.

This tracking dog is hot on the trail.

EARTHDOG TESTS FOR SMALL TERRIERS AND DACHSHUNDS

These tests are open to Australian, Bedlington, Border, Cairn, Dandie Dinmont, Smooth and Wire Fox, Lakeland, Norfolk, Norwich, Scottish, Sealyham, Skye, Welsh and West Highland White Terriers as well as Dachshunds. The dogs need no prior training for this terrier sport. There is a qualifying test on the day of the event, so dog and handler learn the rules on the spot. These tests, or "digs," sometimes end with informal races in the late afternoon.

133

Enjoying Your
Dog

Here are some of the extracurricular obedience and racing activities that are not regulated by the AKC or UKC, but are generally run by clubs or a group of dog fanciers and are often open to all.

Canine Freestyle This activity is something new on the scene and is variously likened to dancing, dressage or ice skating. It is meant to show the athleticism of the dog, but also requires showmanship on the part of the dog's handler. If you and your dog like to ham it up for friends, you might want to look into freestyle.

Lure coursing lets sighthounds do what they do best—run!

Scent Hurdle Racing Scent hurdle racing is purely a fun activity sponsored by obedience clubs with members forming competing teams. The height of the hurdles is based on the size of the shortest dog on the team. On a signal, one team dog is released on each of two side-by-side courses and must clear every hurdle before picking up its own dumbbell from a platform and returning over the jumps to the handler. As each dog returns, the next on that team is sent. Of course, that is what the dogs are supposed to do. When the dogs improvise (going under or around the hurdles, stealing another dog's dumbbell, and so forth), it no doubt frustrates the handlers, but just adds to the fun for everyone else.

Flyball This type of racing is similar, but after negotiating the four hurdles, the dog comes to a flyball box, steps on a lever that releases a tennis ball into the air, catches the ball and returns over the hurdles to the starting point. This game also becomes extremely fun for spectators because the dogs sometimes cheat by catching a ball released by the dog in the next lane. Three titles can be earned—Flyball Dog (F.D.), Flyball Dog Excellent (F.D.X.) and Flyball Dog Champion (Fb.D.Ch.)—all awarded by the North American Flyball Association, Inc.

Dogsledding The name conjures up the Rocky Mountains or the frigid North, but you can find dogsled clubs in such unlikely spots as Maryland, North Carolina and Virginia! Dogsledding is primarily for the Nordic breeds such as the Alaskan Malamutes, Siberian Huskies and Samoyeds, but other breeds can try. There are some practical backyard applications to this sport, too. With parental supervision, almost any strong dog could pull a child's sled.

Coming over the A-frame on an agility course.

These are just some of the many recreational ways you can get to know and understand your multifaceted dog better and have fun doing it.

chapter 10

Your Dog
and your
Family

by Bardi McLennan

Adding a dog automatically increases your family by one, no matter whether you live alone in an apartment or are part of a mother, father and six kids household. The single-person family is fair game for numerous and varied canine misconceptions as to who is dog and who pays the bills, whereas a dog in a houseful of children will consider himself to be just one of the gang, littermates all. One dog and one child may give a dog reason to believe they are both kids or both dogs.

Either interpretation requires parental supervision and sometimes speedy intervention.

As soon as one paw goes through the door into your home, Rufus (or Rufina) has to make many adjustments to become a part of your family. Your job is to make him fit in as painlessly as possible. An older dog may have some frame of reference from past experience, but to a 10-week-old puppy, everything is brand new: people, furniture, stairs, when and where people eat, sleep or watch TV, his own place and everyone else's space, smells, sounds, outdoors—everything!

Puppies, and newly acquired dogs of any age, do not need what we think of as "freedom." If you leave a new dog or puppy loose in the house, you will almost certainly return to chaotic destruction and the dog will forever after equate your homecoming with a time of punishment to be dreaded. It is unfair to give your dog what amounts to "freedom to get into trouble." Instead, confine him to a crate for brief periods of your absence (up to three or four hours) and, for the long haul, a workday for example, confine him to one untrashable area with his own toys, a bowl of water and a radio left on (low) in another room.

Lots of pets get along with each other just fine.

For the first few days, when not confined, put Rufus on a long leash tied to your wrist or waist. This umbilical cord method enables the dog to learn all about you from your body language and voice, and to learn by his own actions which things in the house are NO! and which ones are rewarded by "Good dog." Housetraining will be easier with the pup always by your side. Speaking of which, accidents do happen. That goal of "completely housetrained" takes up to a year, or the length of time it takes the pup to mature.

The All-Adult Family

Most dogs in an adults-only household today are likely to be latchkey pets, with no one home all day but the dog. When you return after a tough day on the job, the dog can and should be your relaxation therapy. But going home can instead be a daily frustration.

Separation anxiety is a very common problem for the dog in a working household. It may begin with whines and barks of loneliness, but it will soon escalate into a frenzied destruction derby. That is why it is so important to set aside the time to teach a dog to relax when left alone in his confined area and to understand that he can trust you to return.

Let the dog get used to your work schedule in easy stages. Confine him to one room and go in and out of that room over and over again. Be casual about it. No physical, voice or eye contact. When the pup no longer even notices your comings and goings, leave the house for varying lengths of time, returning to stay home for a few minutes and gradually increasing the time away. This training can take days, but the dog is learning that you haven't left him forever and that he can trust you.

Any time you leave the dog, but especially during this training period, be casual about your departure. No anxiety-building fond farewells. Just "Bye" and go! Remember the "Good dog" when you return to find everything more or less as you left it.

If things are a mess (or even a disaster) when you return, greet the dog, take him outside to eliminate, and then put him in his crate while you clean up. Rant and rave in the shower! *Do not* punish the dog. You were not there when it happened, and the rule is: Only punish as you catch the dog in the act of wrongdoing. Obviously, it makes sense to get your latchkey puppy when you'll have a week or two to spend on these training essentials.

Family weekend activities should include Rufus whenever possible. Depending on the pup's age, now is the time for a long walk in the park, playtime in the backyard, a hike in the woods. Socializing is as important as health care, good food and physical exercise, so visiting Aunt Emma or Uncle Harry and the next-door neighbor's dog or cat is essential to developing an outgoing, friendly temperament in your pet.

If you are a single adult, socializing Rufus at home and away will prevent him from becoming overly protective of you (or just overly attached) and will also prevent such behavioral problems as dominance or fear of strangers.

Babies

Whether already here or on the way, babies figure larger than life in the eyes of a dog. If the dog is there first, let him in on all your baby preparations in the house. When baby arrives, let Rufus sniff any item of clothing that has been on the baby before Junior comes home. Then let Mom greet the dog first before introducing the new family member. Hold the baby down for the dog to see and sniff, but make sure someone's holding the dog on lead in case of any sudden moves. Don't play keep-away or tease the dog with the baby, which only invites undesirable jumping up.

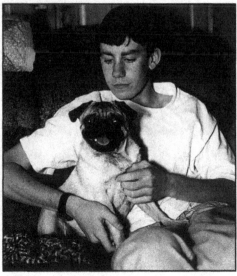

The dog and the baby are "family," and for starters can be treated almost as equals. Things rapidly change, however, especially when baby takes to creeping around on all fours on the dog's turf or, better yet, has yummy pudding all over her face and hands! That's when a lot of things in the dog's and baby's lives become more separate than equal.

Dogs are perfect confidants.

Toddlers make terrible dog owners, but if you can't avoid the combination, use patient discipline (that is, positive teaching rather than punishment), and use time-outs before you run out of patience.

A dog and a baby (or toddler, or an assertive young child) should never be left alone together. Take the dog with you or confine him. With a baby or youngsters in the house, you'll have plenty of use for that wonderful canine safety device called a crate!

Young Children

Any dog in a house with kids will behave pretty much as the kids do, good or bad. But even good dogs and good children can get into trouble when play becomes rowdy and active.

Legs bobbing up and down, shrill voices screeching, a ball hurtling overhead, all add up to exuberant frustration for a dog who's just trying to be part of the gang. In a pack of puppies, any legs or toys being chased would be caught by a set of teeth, and all the pups involved would understand that is how the game is played. Kids do not understand this, nor do parents tolerate it. Bring Rufus indoors before you have reason to regret it. This is time-out, not a punishment.

Teach children how to play nicely with a puppy.

You can explain the situation to the children and tell them they must play quieter games until the puppy learns not to grab them with his mouth. Unfortunately, you can't explain it that easily to the dog. With adult supervision, they will learn how to play together.

Young children love to tease. Sticking their faces or wiggling their hands or fingers in the dog's face is teasing. To another person it might be just annoying, but it is threatening to a dog. There's another difference: We can make the child stop by an explanation, but the only way a dog can stop it is with a warning growl and then with teeth. Teasing is the major cause of children being bitten by their pets. Treat it seriously.

Older Children

The best age for a child to get a first dog is between the ages of 8 and 12. That's when kids are able to accept some real responsibility for their pet. Even so, take the child's vow of "I will never *ever* forget to feed (brush, walk, etc.) the dog" for what it's worth: a child's good intention at that moment. Most kids today have extra lessons, soccer practice, Little League, ballet, and so forth piled on top of school schedules. There will be many times when Mom will have to come to the dog's rescue. "I walked the dog for you so you can set the table for me" is one way to get around a missed appointment without laying on blame or guilt.

Kids in this age group make excellent obedience train- ers because they are into the teaching/learning process themselves and they lack the self-consciousness of adults. Attending a dog show is something the whole family can enjoy, and watching Junior Showmanship may catch the eye of the kids. Older children can begin to get involved in many of the recreational activ- ities that were reviewed in the previous chapter. Some of the agility obstacles, for example, can be set up in the backyard as a family project (with an adult making sure all the equipment is safe and secure for the dog).

Older kids are also beginning to look to the future, and may envision themselves as veterinarians or train- ers or show dog handlers or writers of the next Lassie best-seller. Dogs are perfect confidants for these dreams. They won't tell a soul.

Other Pets

Introduce all pets tactfully. In a dog/cat situation, hold the dog, not the cat. Let two dogs meet on neutral turf—a stroll in the park or a walk down the street— with both on loose leads to permit all the normal canine ways of saying hello, including routine sniffing, circling, more sniffing, and so on. Small creatures such as hamsters, chinchillas or mice must be kept safe from their natural predators (dogs and cats).

Festive Family Occasions

Parties are great for people, but not necessarily for puppies. Until all the guests have arrived, put the dog in his crate or in a room where he won't be disturbed. A socialized dog can join the fun later as long as he's not underfoot, annoying guests or into the hors d'oeuvres.

There are a few dangers to consider, too. Doors opening and closing can allow a puppy to slip out unnoticed in the confusion, and you'll be organizing a search party instead of playing host or hostess. Party food and buffet service are not for dogs. Let Rufus party in his crate with a nice big dog biscuit.

At Christmas time, not only are tree decorations dangerous and breakable (and perhaps family heirlooms), but extreme caution should be taken with the lights, cords and outlets for the tree lights and any other festive lighting. Occasionally a dog lifts a leg, ignoring the fact that the tree is indoors. To avoid this, use a canine repellent, made for gardens, on the tree. Or keep him out of the tree room unless supervised. And whatever you do, *don't* invite trouble by hanging his toys on the tree!

Car Travel

Before you plan a vacation by car or RV with Rufus, be sure he enjoys car travel. Nothing spoils a holiday quicker than a carsick dog! Work within the dog's comfort level. Get in the car with the dog in his crate or attached to a canine car safety belt and just sit there until he relaxes. That's all. Next time, get in the car, turn on the engine and go nowhere. Just sit. When that is okay, turn on the engine and go around the block. Now you can go for a ride and include a stop where you get out, leaving the dog for a minute or two.

On a warm day, always park in the shade and leave windows open several inches. And return quickly. It only takes 10 minutes for a car to become an overheated steel death trap.

Motel or Pet Motel?

Not all motels or hotels accept pets, but you have a much better choice today than even a few years ago. To find a dog-friendly lodging, look at *On the Road Again With Man's Best Friend*, a series of directories that detail bed and breakfasts, inns, family resorts and other hotels/motels. Some places require a refundable deposit to cover any damage incurred by the dog. More B&Bs accept pets now, but some restrict the size.

If taking Rufus with you is not feasible, check out boarding kennels in your area. Your veterinarian may offer this service, or recommend a kennel or two he or she is familiar with. Go see the facilities for yourself, ask about exercise, diet, housing, and so on. Or, if you'd rather have Rufus stay home, look into bonded petsitters, many of whom will also bring in the mail and water your plants.

chapter 11

Your Dog
and your
Community

by Bardi McLennan

Step outside your home with your dog and you are no longer just family, you are both part of your community. This is when the phrase "responsible pet ownership" takes on serious implications. For starters, it means you pick up after your dog—not just occasionally, but every time your dog eliminates away from home. That means you have joined the Plastic Baggy Brigade! You always have plastic sandwich bags in your pocket and several in the car. It means you teach your kids how to use them, too. If you think this is "yucky," just imagine what the person (a non-doggy person) who inadvertently steps in the mess thinks!

Your responsibility extends to your neighbors: To their ears (no annoying barking); to their property (their garbage, their lawn, their flower beds, their cat—especially their cat); to their kids (on bikes, at play); to their kids' toys and sports equipment.

There are numerous dog-related laws, ranging from simple dog licensing and leash laws to those holding you liable for any physical injury or property damage done by your dog. These laws are in place to protect everyone in the community, including you and your dog. There are town ordinances and state laws which are by no means the same in all towns or all states. Ignorance of the law won't get you off the hook. The time to find out what the laws are where you live is now.

Dressing your dog up makes him appealing to strangers.

Be sure your dog's license is current. This is not just a good local ordinance, it can make the difference between finding your lost dog or not. Many states now require proof of rabies vaccination and that the dog has been spayed or neutered before issuing a license. At the same time, keep up the dog's annual immunizations.

Never let your dog run loose in the neighborhood. This will not only keep you on the right side of the leash law, it's the outdoor version of the rule about not giving your dog "freedom to get into trouble."

Good Canine Citizen

Sometimes it's hard for a dog's owner to assess whether or not the dog is sufficiently socialized to be accepted by the community at large. Does Rufus or Rufina display good, controlled behavior in public? The AKC's Canine Good Citizen program is available through many dog organizations. If your dog passes the test, the title "CGC" is earned.

The overall purpose is to turn your dog into a good neighbor and to teach you about your responsibility to your community as a dog owner. Here are the ten things your dog must do willingly:

1. Allow a stranger to handle him or her as a groomer or veterinarian would.
2. Accept a stranger stopping to chat with you.
3. Walk nicely on a loose lead.
4. Walk calmly through a crowd.
5. Sit and be petted by a stranger.
6. Sit and down on command.
7. Stay put when you move away.
8. Casually greet another dog.
9. React confidently to distractions.
10. Accept being tied up in a strange place and left alone for a few minutes.

Schools and Dogs

Schools are getting involved with pet ownership on an educational level. It has been proven that children who are kind to animals are humane in their attitude toward other people as adults.

A dog is a child's best friend, and so children are often primary pet owners, if not the primary caregivers. Unfortunately, they are also the ones most often bitten by dogs. This occurs due to a lack of understanding that pets, no matter how sweet, cuddly and loving, are still animals. Schools, along with parents, dog clubs, dog fanciers and the AKC, are working to change all that with video programs for children not only in grade school, but in the nursery school and pre-kindergarten age group. Teaching youngsters how to be responsible dog owners is important community work. When your dog has a CGC, volunteer to take part in an educational classroom event put on by your dog club.

Boy Scout Merit Badge

A Merit Badge for Dog Care can be earned by any Boy Scout ages 11 to 18. The requirements are not easy, but amount to a complete course in responsible dog care and general ownership. Here are just a few of the things a Scout must do to earn that badge:

Point out ten parts of the dog using the correct names.

Give a report (signed by parent or guardian) on your care of the dog (feeding, food used, housing, exercising, grooming and bathing), plus what has been done to keep the dog healthy.

Explain the right way to obedience train a dog, and demonstrate three comments.

Several of the requirements have to do with health care, including first aid, handling a hurt dog, and the dangers of home treatment for a serious ailment.

The final requirement is to know the local laws and ordinances involving dogs.

There are similar programs for Girl Scouts and 4-H members.

Local Clubs

Local dog clubs are no longer in existence just to put on a yearly dog show. Today, they are apt to be the hub of the community's involvement with pets. Dog clubs conduct educational forums with big-name speakers, stage demonstrations of canine talent in a busy mall and take dogs of various breeds to schools for class-room discussion.

The quickest way to feel accepted as a member in a club is to volunteer your services! Offer to help with something—anything—and watch your popularity (and your interest) grow.

Therapy Dogs

Once your dog has earned that essential CGC and reliably demonstrates a steady, calm temperament, you could look into what therapy dogs are doing in your area.

Therapy dogs go with their owners to visit patients at hospitals or nursing homes, generally remaining on leash but able to coax a pat from a stiffened hand, a smile from a blank face, a few words from sealed lips or a hug from someone in need of love.

Nursing homes cover a wide range of patient care. Some specialize in care of the elderly, some in the treatment of specific illnesses, some in physical therapy. Children's facilities also welcome visits from trained therapy dogs for boosting morale in their pediatric patients. Hospice care for the terminally ill and the at-home care of AIDS patients are other areas where this canine visiting is desperately needed. Therapy dog training comes first.

Your dog can make a difference in lots of lives.

There is a lot more involved than just taking your nice friendly pooch to someone's bedside. Doing therapy dog work involves your own emotional stability as well as that of your dog. But once you have met all the requirements for this work, making the rounds once a week or once a month with your therapy dog is possibly the most rewarding of all community activities.

Disaster Aid

This community service is definitely not for everyone, partly because it is time-consuming. The initial training is rigorous, and there can be no let-up in the continuing workouts, because members are on call 24 hours a day to go wherever they are needed at a moment's notice. But if you think you would like to be able to assist in a disaster, look into search-and-rescue work. The network of search-and-rescue volunteers is worldwide, and all members of the American Rescue Dog Association (ARDA) who are qualified to do this work are volunteers who train and maintain their own dogs.

Physical Aid

Most people are familiar with Seeing Eye dogs, which serve as blind people's eyes, but not with all the other work that dogs are trained to do to assist the disabled. Dogs are also specially trained to pull wheelchairs, carry school books, pick up dropped objects, open and close doors. Some also are ears for the deaf. All these assistance-trained dogs, by the way, are allowed anywhere "No Pet" signs exist (as are therapy dogs when properly identified). Getting started in any of this fascinating work requires a background in dog training and canine behavior, but there are also volunteer jobs ranging from answering the phone to cleaning out kennels to providing a foster home for a puppy. You have only to ask.

Making the rounds with your therapy dog can be very rewarding.

part four

Beyond
the
Basics

chapter 12

Recommended Reading

Books

ABOUT HEALTH CARE

Ackerman, Lowell. *Guide to Skin and Haircoat Problems in Dogs*. Loveland, Colo.: Alpine Publications, 1994.

Alderton, David. *The Dog Care Manual*. Hauppauge, N.Y.: Barron's Educational Series, Inc., 1986.

American Kennel Club. *American Kennel Club Dog Care and Training*. New York: Howell Book House, 1991.

Bamberger, Michelle, DVM. *Help! The Quick Guide to First Aid for Your Dog*. New York: Howell Book House, 1995.

Carlson, Delbert, DVM, and James Giffin, MD. *Dog Owner's Home Veterinary Handbook*. New York: Howell Book House, 1992.

DeBitetto, James, DVM, and Sarah Hodgson. *You & Your Puppy*. New York: Howell Book House, 1995.

Humphries, Jim, DVM. *Dr. Jim's Animal Clinic for Dogs*. New York: Howell Book House, 1994.

McGinnis, Terri. *The Well Dog Book*. New York: Random House, 1991.

Pitcairn, Richard and Susan. *Natural Health for Dogs*. Emmaus, Pa.: Rodale Press, 1982.

ABOUT DOG SHOWS

Hall, Lynn. *Dog Showing for Beginners*. New York: Howell Book House, 1994.

Nichols, Virginia Tuck. *How to Show Your Own Dog*. Neptune, N. J.: TFH, 1970.

Vanacore, Connie. *Dog Showing, An Owner's Guide*. New York: Howell Book House, 1990.

ABOUT TRAINING

Ammen, Amy. *Training in No Time.* New York: Howell Book House, 1995.

Baer, Ted. *Communicating With Your Dog.* Hauppauge, N.Y.: Barron's Educational Series, Inc., 1989.

Benjamin, Carol Lea. *Dog Problems.* New York: Howell Book House, 1989.

Benjamin, Carol Lea. *Dog Training for Kids.* New York: Howell Book House, 1988.

Benjamin, Carol Lea. *Mother Knows Best.* New York: Howell Book House, 1985.

Benjamin, Carol Lea. *Surviving Your Dog's Adolescence.* New York: Howell Book House, 1993.

Bohnenkamp, Gwen. *Manners for the Modern Dog.* San Francisco: Perfect Paws, 1990.

Dibra, Bashkim. *Dog Training by Bash.* New York: Dell, 1992.

Dunbar, Ian, PhD, MRCVS. *Dr. Dunbar's Good Little Dog Book,* James & Kenneth Publishers, 2140 Shattuck Ave. #2406, Berkeley, Calif. 94704. (510) 658–8588. Order from the publisher.

Dunbar, Ian, PhD, MRCVS. *How to Teach a New Dog Old Tricks,* James & Kenneth Publishers. Order from the publisher; address above.

Dunbar, Ian, PhD, MRCVS, and Gwen Bohnenkamp. Booklets on *Preventing Aggression; Housetraining; Chewing; Digging; Barking; Socialization; Fearfulness; and Fighting,* James & Kenneth Publishers. Order from the publisher; address above.

Evans, Job Michael. *People, Pooches and Problems.* New York: Howell Book House, 1991.

Kilcommons, Brian and Sarah Wilson. *Good Owners, Great Dogs.* New York: Warner Books, 1992.

McMains, Joel M. *Dog Logic—Companion Obedience.* New York: Howell Book House, 1992.

Rutherford, Clarice and David H. Neil, MRCVS. *How to Raise a Puppy You Can Live With.* Loveland, Colo.: Alpine Publications, 1982.

Volhard, Jack and Melissa Bartlett. *What All Good Dogs Should Know: The Sensible Way to Train.* New York: Howell Book House, 1991.

ABOUT BREEDING

Harris, Beth J. Finder. *Breeding a Litter, The Complete Book of Prenatal and Postnatal Care.* New York: Howell Book House, 1983.

Holst, Phyllis, DVM. *Canine Reproduction.* Loveland, Colo.: Alpine Publications, 1985.

Beyond the Basics

Walkowicz, Chris and Bonnie Wilcox, DVM. *Successful Dog Breeding, The Complete Handbook of Canine Midwifery*. New York: Howell Book House, 1994.

ABOUT ACTIVITIES

American Rescue Dog Association. *Search and Rescue Dogs*. New York: Howell Book House, 1991.

Barwig, Susan and Stewart Hilliard. *Schutzhund*. New York: Howell Book House, 1991.

Beaman, Arthur S. *Lure Coursing*. New York: Howell Book House, 1994.

Daniels, Julie. *Enjoying Dog Agility—From Backyard to Competition*. New York: Doral Publishing, 1990.

Davis, Kathy Diamond. *Therapy Dogs*. New York: Howell Book House, 1992.

Gallup, Davis Anne. *Running With Man's Best Friend*. Loveland, Colo.: Alpine Publications, 1986.

Habgood, Dawn and Robert. *On the Road Again With Man's Best Friend*. New England, Mid-Atlantic, West Coast and Southeast editions. Selective guides to area bed and breakfasts, inns, hotels and resorts that welcome guests and their dogs. New York: Howell Book House, 1995.

Holland, Vergil S. *Herding Dogs*. New York: Howell Book House, 1994.

LaBelle, Charlene G. *Backpacking With Your Dog*. Loveland, Colo.: Alpine Publications, 1993.

Simmons-Moake, Jane. *Agility Training, The Fun Sport for All Dogs*. New York: Howell Book House, 1991.

Spencer, James B. *Hup! Training Flushing Spaniels the American Way*. New York: Howell Book House, 1992.

Spencer, James B. *Point! Training the All-Seasons Birddog*. New York: Howell Book House, 1995.

Tarrant, Bill. *Training the Hunting Retriever*. New York: Howell Book House, 1991.

Volhard, Jack and Wendy. *The Canine Good Citizen*. New York: Howell Book House, 1994.

General Titles

Haggerty, Captain Arthur J. *How to Get Your Pet Into Show Business*. New York: Howell Book House, 1994.

McLennan, Bardi. *Dogs and Kids, Parenting Tips*. New York: Howell Book House, 1993.

Moran, Patti J. *Pet Sitting for Profit, A Complete Manual for Professional Success*. New York: Howell Book House, 1992.

Scalisi, Danny and Libby Moses. *When Rover Just Won't Do, Over 2,000 Suggestions for Naming Your Dog*. New York: Howell Book House, 1993.

Sife, Wallace, PhD. *The Loss of a Pet*. New York: Howell Book House, 1993.

Wrede, Barbara J. *Civilizing Your Puppy*. Hauppauge, N.Y.: Barron's Educational Series, 1992.

Magazines

The AKC GAZETTE, The Official Journal for the Sport of Purebred Dogs. American Kennel Club, 51 Madison Ave., New York, NY.

Bloodlines Journal. United Kennel Club, 100 E. Kilgore Rd., Kalamazoo, MI.

Dog Fancy. Fancy Publications, 3 Burroughs, Irvine, CA 92718

Dog World. Maclean Hunter Publishing Corp., 29 N. Wacker Dr., Chicago, IL 60606.

Videos

"SIRIUS Puppy Training," by Ian Dunbar, PhD, MRCVS. James & Kenneth Publishers, 2140 Shattuck Ave. #2406, Berkeley, CA 94704. Order from the publisher.

"Training the Companion Dog," from Dr. Dunbar's British TV Series, James & Kenneth Publishers. (See address above).

The American Kennel Club produces videos on every breed of dog, as well as on hunting tests, field trials and other areas of interest to purebred dog owners. For more information, write to AKC/Video Fulfillment, 5580 Centerview Dr., Suite 200, Raleigh, NC 27606.

chapter 13

Resources

Breed Clubs

Every breed recognized by the American Kennel Club has a national (parent) club. National clubs are a great source of information on your breed. You can get the name of the secretary of the club by contacting:

The American Kennel Club
51 Madison Avenue
New York, NY 10010
(212) 696-8200

There are also numerous all-breed, individual breed, obedience, hunting and other special-interest dog clubs across the country. The American Kennel Club can provide you with a geographical list of clubs to find ones in your area. Contact them at the above address.

Registry Organizations

Registry organizations register purebred dogs. The American Kennel Club is the oldest and largest in this country, and currently recognizes over 130 breeds. The United Kennel Club registers some breeds the AKC doesn't (including the American Pit Bull Terrier and the Miniature Fox Terrier) as well as many of the same breeds. The others included here are for your reference; the AKC can provide you with a list of foreign registries.

American Kennel Club
51 Madison Avenue
New York, NY 10010

United Kennel Club (UKC)
100 E. Kilgore Road
Kalamazoo, MI 49001-5598

American Dog Breeders Assn.
P.O. Box 1771
Salt Lake City, UT 84110
(Registers American Pit Bull Terriers)

Canadian Kennel Club
89 Skyway Avenue
Etobicoke, Ontario
Canada M9W 6R4

National Stock Dog Registry
P.O. Box 402
Butler, IN 46721
(Registers working stock dogs)

Orthopedic Foundation for Animals (OFA)
2300 E. Nifong Blvd.
Columbia, MO 65201-3856
(Hip registry)

Activity Clubs

Write to these organizations for information on the
activities they sponsor.

American Kennel Club
51 Madison Avenue
New York, NY 10010
(Conformation Shows, Obedience Trials, Field
Trials and Hunting Tests, Agility, Canine Good

Citizen, Lure Coursing, Herding, Tracking,
Earthdog Tests, Coonhunting.)

United Kennel Club
100 E. Kilgore Road
Kalamazoo, MI 49001-5598
(Conformation Shows, Obedience Trials, Agility,
Hunting for Various Breeds, Terrier Trials and
more.)

North American Flyball Assn.
1342 Jeff St.
Ypsilanti, MI 48198

International Sled Dog Racing Assn.
P.O. Box 446
Norman, ID 83848-0446

North American Working Dog Assn., Inc.
Southcast Kreisgruppe
P.O. Box 833
Brunswick, GA 31521

Trainers

Association of Pet Dog Trainers
P.O. Box 3734
Salinas, CA 93912
(408) 663–9257

American Dog Trainers' Network
161 West 4th St.
New York, NY 10014
(212) 727–7257

**National Association of Dog Obedience
Instructors**
2286 East Steel Rd.
St. Johns, MI 48879

Associations

American Dog Owners Assn.
1654 Columbia Tpk.
Castleton, NY 12033
(Combats anti-dog legislation)

Delta Society
P.O. Box 1080
Renton, WA 98057-1080
(Promotes the human/animal bond through
pet-assisted therapy and other programs)

Dog Writers Assn. of America (DWAA)
Sally Cooper, Secy.
222 Woodchuck Ln.
Harwinton, CT 06791

National Assn. for Search and Rescue (NASAR)
P.O. Box 3709
Fairfax, VA 22038

Therapy Dogs International
1536 Morris Place
Hillside, NJ 07205

CPSIA information can be obtained
at www.ICGtesting.com
Printed in the USA
LVHW081223180521
687768LV00003B/21